NORTH-WEST PASSAGE

WILLY DE ROOS

North-West Passage

Translated from the French
by Bruce Penman

Foreword by
Rear-Admiral G. S. Ritchie, CB, DSC
Hydrographer of the Navy (1966–71)
President, Directing Committee,
International Hydrographic Bureau

HOLLIS & CARTER
LONDON   SYDNEY
TORONTO

To the memory of my father,
To my family,
To my children,
To her.

British Library Cataloguing
in Publication Data
Roos, Willy de
North-West Passage.
1. Northwest passage
2. Williwaw (*Boat*)
I. Title
910′.09′16327   G700   1977
ISBN 0–370–30263–X

© Librairie Arthaud, Paris, 1979
English translation © The Bodley Head Ltd. 1980
Foreword © G. S. Ritchie 1980
Printed in Great Britain for
Hollis & Carter
an associate company of
The Bodley Head Ltd.
9 Bow Street, London WC2E 7AL
by Redwood Burn Ltd
Trowbridge & Esher
Set in Monotype Imprint
by Gloucester Typesetting Co. Ltd
First published in Great Britain 1980

CONTENTS

Illustrations

Maps

Maps drawn by Ken Jordan

FOREWORD
by Rear-Admiral G. S. Ritchie. C.B., D.S.C.

In the early sixteenth century, when the Ottoman Turks dominated the caravan routes from the East to the shores of the Mediterranean, and the newly discovered sea routes—southwards round Africa or through Magellan's Straits—were under the virtual control of the Portuguese and the Spanish, northern European states turned their attention to the finding of a North-East or North-West Passage. The supply of spices and other riches from the Orient had become essential to European living.

Explorations in search of a North-West Passage may be said to have begun with three voyages led by Frobisher in the 1570s, followed by three voyages by Davis a decade later, and Hudson's voyages in the early years of the seventeenth century, but in 1631 Luke Foxe and Thomas James finally disproved the existence of a passage westwards from Hudson's Bay.

Apart from Captain Cook's attempt in 1778 to find a passage eastwards from the North Pacific no concerted efforts were made again until after the Napoleonic Wars. By then the commercial necessity had declined but there were both naval officers and civilians in England who believed whole-heartedly that the resources of a victorious Navy should, with the coming of peace, be devoted to geographical exploration. Under the guidance of John Barrow, the Second Secretary of the Admiralty, the first of many British naval expeditions set out in 1818. The area of search was now moved far to the north, probing westwards from Lancaster Sound.

The loss of *Erebus* and *Terror* with their entire ships' companies in 1847/48, far from halting arctic exploration, gave it increased impetus as the many search expeditions set out. The North-West Passage was 'attacked' from both east and west. This second great assault may be said to have culminated in April 1853 when Lieutenant Pim of the *Herald*, which was wintering at Melville Island, travelled westwards on foot across the sea-ice and reached *Investigator* which, under Commander McClure, had entered the Arctic through the Bering Strait and had been held fast in the ice on the north coast of Banks Island for the past three winters. This was the first time that two parties, one from the east and one from the west, had met across the arctic seas, and was as near as anyone ever came in the nineteenth century to finding a North-West sea passage.

At last, in the earliest years of the twentieth century, the Norwegian explorer Amundsen was successful. With six companions, in the 50-ton fishing vessel, *Gjøa* fitted with an auxiliary engine, he set out on the route thought to have been taken by Sir John Franklin with *Erebus* and *Terror*. He wintered for two seasons in Gjøa Haven on the east coast of King William Island and finally reached the Pacific in August 1906. Then in the 1940s Sergeant Larsen of the Royal Canadian Mounted Police in *St. Roch*, a specially-built two-masted schooner with auxiliary engine, not only repeated Amundsen's success but also made the passage from west to east.

Willy de Roos is an introspective but very practical man, who feels deeply that he is a part of natural creation. He took to the sea at the age of fifty, and whilst sailing his 13-metre steel-hulled ketch *Williwaw* round the world was overcome by an ambition to sail his boat through the North-West Passage. Accordingly when back on shore he began to make detailed preparations.

Pilotage best describes the type of navigation required to weave through labyrinths of islands and ever-changing mazes of pack-ice that an arctic voyage in a small boat entails. The basis of pilotage is historical input; long before charts were known in northern European waters seamen who embarked on coastal voyages relied upon descriptions of headlands to be steered for, shallows to be avoided, and safe anchorages: information handed down from one generation of seamen to the next by word of mouth or in rudimentary sketch books. Willy de Roos set about providing himself with this type of information by reading the many available accounts by earlier arctic voyagers from Davis in the sixteenth century to Larsen in the twentieth. De Roos was acutely aware from his reading of where the more treacherous areas of ice were to be expected, where bays best sheltered from moving pack-ice were to be found and where submerged rocks and reefs had been encountered by his predecessors. Little of such information is yet to be found on arctic charts.

One dark night, with a rising gale and falling snow, *Williwaw* had to seek refuge in Pasley Bay, where Larsen's *St. Roch* had been iced in for eleven months in 1941/42. Larsen had damaged his vessel's keel on a reef, the position of which within the bay he had accurately described in his report. Armed as he was with this information, de Roos, using his radar and echo-sounder, brought the ketch safely to anchor only a few metres from the reef. It is after recounting this experience that the author pays tribute to the early explorers, many of whom he names—'I personally owe them a great deal; it is they who initiated me into arctic navigation'.

The planning and the execution of the voyage provide a superb example of the art of pilotage which might well be followed by others in command of much larger vessels when faced with the need to make a passage through confined waters. Perhaps Willy de Roos struck a lucky year enabling him to make the voyage from the Atlantic to the Pacific without having to winter in the Arctic, but it was his foreknowledge of the many alternatives that might become open to him that enabled him to snatch opportunities when they came, however exhausted and weary he might be.

The author tells his tale in a very personal yet matter-of-fact way, so that in reading the book I felt dejected at every set-back, elated by each recovery and nervously excited during the last race against the ice across the Beaufort Sea. The pack was closing in towards the shores of Alaska as September drew on, thus making a safe arrival at Point Barrow uncertain until almost the final day of the passage. His ultimate success was for Willy de Roos the attainment of the goal towards which he struggled so hard and so long.

G. S. Ritchie

Vocation

The love of sailing came into my life rather late. I must have been nearly thirty-five when I climbed on board a yacht for the first time. I had had several other hobbies since the end of the 1939–1945 war during which I had successively been a political prisoner, an escaped prisoner on the run, a member of the Maquis and, finally, a member of the Army of Liberation. When the fighting was over, I got married. The war had robbed me of part of my youth, and I was simultaneously haunted by the fear of wasting my adult life and by the need to recapture the youthful years that I had missed.

Ever since, my personality has been shaped by these factors. I have been lucky enough to be able to achieve a harmonious synthesis of my two aspirations, and to find the justification for my adult universe in my nostalgia for youth. This enabled me to alternate between the roles of managing director and teenager, to put my heart into my business and to be businesslike about what lay closest to my heart.

The first sport I took up was motorcycling. I competed for about ten years, at the end of which I broke my shoulder in an accident. My wife had been pressing me to give it up—we had four little daughters to provide for—and I promised to find a less violent hobby.

When my convalescence was over, I went to the other extreme and became a billiards enthusiast. But this sport soon proved to be much more deleterious than it seemed. Billiards is played in a café, in the evening or sometimes at night, and before long I was never at home. This was too much for my wife, who insisted that I must choose a hobby which I could pursue under my own roof. This, I thought, was not a bad idea. A relic of my childhood still lurked somewhere inside me—the regret that I had never owned a miniature railway. Steam locomotives had always fascinated me: I love the big wheels, the visible movement of the external connecting-rods, the panting sound of the release-valve, the air of tranquil strength, and the black-faced driver and fireman with their red scarves. The prospect of building a miniature railway enchanted me; I was good with my hands, and my training in electro-mechanics guaranteed that I would be able to put together an interesting infrastructure. The two big lofts of our house were rapidly transformed into a busy workshop where stations, tunnels, bridges and permanent ways were constructed.

Coming home at the end of my working day, I was impatient to get back to my trains—and also, no doubt, the dreams associated with them. And so I passed the best part of my free time in the loft; when my wife shouted up the ladder to tell me that supper was ready, I scarcely heard her. Bertha soon grew tired of my passion for the upper regions, all the more so because the children also preferred the atmosphere of the loft. This was better suited to the carefree mind of childhood than the atmosphere of the ground floor, where they left their homework and exercise books when they came up to join me. To preserve the unity of the family, I tried to interest Bertha in my leisure occupations.

I was quite prepared to make sacrifices, but not to live a life of tedium. For me, inactivity is the worst frustration.

So I decided to take up art—which is an activity open to both sexes if ever there was one—and became a weekend painter. Every Sunday I took my wife and children and my painting equipment, and set out into the surrounding countryside, looking for a picturesque spot. Sometimes I would stop the old rattletrap and get everyone out only to discover that the place was not after all sufficiently picturesque, and make everyone pile in again—my wife in a bad temper and my daughters somewhat astonished! These were minor, incidental mistakes, and I could see their funny side. So could the children, who exchanged an occasional sidelong glance of comprehension with me.

It takes a brave man to be a landscape artist! By the time you have put up your easel and opened your paint-box, several inquisitive characters are already looking over your shoulder at the canvas. You pretend to be so taken up with your task that you do not know they are there, but their eyes follow every movement you make, and you are irritated by the persistence with which they stare at you. They also stand too close behind you and get in your way. They prevent you from taking that indispensable step to the rear, from leaning your body back with one arm outstretched to brandish the palette while the other reaches out with the brush as you tilt your head slightly to apply the all-important touch—the touch which, alas, may arouse comment among the spectators. Ah! a word or two about those comments! . . . Uttered in a loud, clear voice, often of a kind which might undermine the most well-founded vocation, they would deal a cruel blow to your self-respect if you were not convinced that the art of today can accommodate the most absurd fantasies—if you did not know that Van Gogh (admittedly in a period of more rigorous standards) was turned down for the Academy. So my answer to the spectators was a show of indifference which was intended to be stoical and impenetrable. Bertha, on the other hand, is always upset by the possibility of ridicule, and she was very embarrassed. There were several occasions when she felt it necessary to seek safety in flight, and after this she refused categorically to come out with me again.

This was annoying; but when I had another look at my pictures, I had to admit that the loss to the world of art would not be irreparable, and I put away my easel for the last time without much regret . . .

In any case, a new factor had come to widen my horizon. Danielle, the eldest of my daughters, had just had her thirteenth birthday; the others, Suzy, Liliane and Martine were not far behind. This meant that the duties of education were becoming more immediate, from my point of view. It must be said, however that our games in the loft had brought us very near together. Up there there was an atmosphere of close friendship—a friendship in which James, our cat, was a full member. I was very fond of him; he was thin and inclined to amorous adventure, which gave me a fellow-feeling for him. He spent a lot of time lazing in the pram which had belonged to Martine, peacefully getting the sleep which he needed after his regular nocturnal excursions. The children made a great fuss of him. James formed the centre for our caresses, and it was in this way that I discovered how very kind my children always were to him. I attached a great deal of importance to this, for, as Gresset says, 'when the heart is kind, anything else can be put right.' I am a great believer in the riches that kindness brings with it, and I have always hoped that my children would have generosity of heart, though it does sometimes make for difficulties in life. What I saw in the loft encouraged me to think that this hope would be fulfilled, and I was very pleased. I firmly believe that it was through our games that I came to know my children, and the 'loft at Rue Langemark', as we later came to call it, is still one of our happiest common memories.

I am no enthusiast for women's lib, as generally understood in our industrialised society, where it is often no more than an excuse for sending women out to work. On the contrary, I am in favour of anything which tends to encourage femininity.

One cannot, alas, arrest the march of progress, even of the most doubtful variety, and I had to accept the necessity of giving my children an education which would prepare them for a possible professional career; but I could not bring myself to neglect for this reason anything which makes up the charm of the feminine character.

I accordingly wanted my children to study music, which is both a means of expression and a sentimental education. So I bought a piano and put the girls down for a course of music lessons. For my own part, to accompany them a little way on this road, I studied the same subject at night-school.

Scales and arpeggios were practised every day. The neighbours complained about it, and my wife, who found her television watching seriously affected, took a violent dislike to our musical interests.

We fought hard for our rights, but in the end we had to give in to pressures which came from all sides. What with neighbours (who are virtually part of the family nowadays because the walls are so thin in a modern building), the attractions of television, the large amount of homework which had to be done and the craze for hi-fi, too many things conspired against us. It is impossible to describe the strain suffered in our time by fathers and mothers who persist in regarding the task of educating their children as a duty and a privilege of their relationship.

I was accordingly appalled by the behaviour of the public authorities, who are not content with ensuring that children get an education, but claim the right to take care of their health and even their moral training, in its most intimate details. The same treatment and same philosophy is prescribed for every child. Thus the loss of family identity precedes the loss of the identity of the individual.

I know very well that all this suits some people; and the more women go out to work, the more of those people there will be. The family nest will cease to exist. And what does that matter after all if not everybody wants it to exist?—if the majority takes a decision, everyone's mind is at rest. A sign of the times . . .

To sum up, my children came home every day full to the brim with ideas with which I could not agree. As I was domiciled in the Flemish part of Belgium (which was once a very hospitable part of the world), I was forbidden to educate my children in French, even after I had moved, for this very reason, into the French-speaking part of the country. Bertha herself is French-speaking and has no knowledge of Flemish; and so it was not long before the children were talking to each other in a language that their mother could not understand. I have always thought that that was disgusting! This was in fact the point at which I resolved to do one thing for myself and for my children—to recover that personal identity which we were losing through our incorporation in a system that was becoming more and more authoritarian.

I must admit that I had little to complain of on the strictly material plane. I was earning a decent living, and I loved my work. But my decision to work double time to get myself out of the 'system' did not cost me much effort. That decision duly bore fruit later on, and I have never for a moment regretted taking it. The following spring, I bought a decked whale-boat. I noticed it one day as I was walking along the Willebroek Canal where it was resting after a fairly long life.

My object was to take it down to the coast and to spend our family holiday on it that summer. Having no experience of the sea, I had asked a friend of mine to come with me as far as the coast, and he had agreed. But unfortunately his wife, though less timid than Bertha, stopped him coming just as we were ready to cast off.

'It's not very difficult,' said my friend, trying to make the best of it, 'the canal won't present any problems, and once you're on the Scheldt you'll see two kinds of buoy—red ones and black ones. All you have to do is to steer between the two rows!'

So I set off on my own. To begin with everything was all right, but suddenly I came across a buoy which was neither red nor black, but green! What could that mean? It had a notice on it, in white letters, but I was too far away to read it. So I steered for it, rounded it, and was horrified to read the word WRECK! I had made a silly mistake: the twisted ironwork of a sunken ship was bristling under my keel, and could easily have holed my hull!

Well, I was lucky enough to stay afloat on that occasion, and it helped me to realise that sailing is a serious matter. Not long afterwards I got my yachtsman's certificate at the Naval School of Ostend. I was hooked.

I have devoted this first chapter to some of my previous experiences because they show that my vocation as a sailor is above all the result of a combination of features in my character, notably a desire to run my own life according to my own logic. This explains my enthusiasm for motorcycling. A motorcyclist racing at top speed is on his own, even if the rails are crowded with spectators. He alone chooses the moment to brake, to swerve, or to accelerate, and he alone accepts responsibility for the consequences of all his decisions.

On this basis, and provided that he does not try to exceed his own limitations, he is behaving in a responsible manner. Whether he is a champion or an ordinary competitor, what matters to him is to know that he can go right to the limits of his capacity without ever exceeding them, and to acquire that self-confidence without which there can be no inner peace.

In the same way, an artist can attain peace by creating a work which expresses his instincts, his inward needs. It would not be right for a man to go outside his own true nature in an attempt to find his personal identity or the limits of his capacity; but I am passionately convinced that every man has at the very least the right to be all that he is capable of being.

In point of fact, our everyday life ought to allow us to carry out our aspirations, and give us a chance to realise ourselves; but the organisation of our society unfortunately takes less and less account of the individual's need to run his own life. As far as I am concerned, my desire for a self-sufficient existence has grown stronger with the years, and this aspiration could only guide me towards a love of exploration in the mountains, in the desert or at sea. There are unfortunately hardly any other openings for a free-ranging spirit.

You already know what happened—the sea took a major part in my life. If my original motivation came about as I have described above, it has been greatly enriched by the passage of the years.

In the following chapters, I shall do my best to let you share what I have learnt from the sea, about the sea and about myself. I shall try to give an account of matters which lie in the no-man's-land between the tangible and the unattainable, without forgetting to evoke a picture of the men and the lands I met along my way.

2

Preparations

The years went by. The idea of sailing round the world had taken clearer shape. My children had grown up; nearly all of them were married, and only Martine was still at home.

I should have preferred not to have set out on my travels while she was still with us, but I was nearly fifty and it seemed to me that the time for decision had come.

I had given myself a push in the right direction a year or two earlier, by starting to collect the necessary equipment; and the yards of Michot Frères at Thuin were quietly and competently getting on with the construction of a thirteen-metre steel ketch, which had been designed for me by Louis Van de Wiele.

After long reflection I finally decided to give up my business. This was a difficult decision, because I was in an excellent line of trade, which assured me of freedom from want. Also the work was agreeable: mutual understanding and a real team spirit made it possible for my turnover to show a steady advance, thanks to my own efforts and those of all my colleagues. With the passage of the years, our relationship had become a very friendly one, and it was not easy to leave those who had worked with me. We had all shared the same wish to earn a decent living for our families, and none of us had ever considered his relative prosperity as an end in itself or as a means of domination. This similar way of looking at things lay at the base of our friendly relationship and, indeed, of the success of our enterprise. It consequently seemed natural to me that the marriage of my children should put an end to an important part of my financial preoccupations; and I therefore felt free to impart a new direction to my life. But I had not yet taken the final step, for giving up business did not only mean leaving safety for the unknown (like a man leaving his warm bed on a winter's morning), but also breaking with long established habits, turning one's back on certain, easy success, deliberately turning over a page of one's life, and substituting a permanent question mark for a fully planned future.

For a long time I found it difficult to take the final step, for the decision seemed to me heavily fraught with consequences. But gradually I came to see that the decision to retire brought with it spiritual safeguards greater than those inherent in my previous situation. Have we not already forgotten our warm bed, as we breathe in the pure air of a winter's morning in the snowy country-side? And can a man believe in himself if he judges himself by the yardstick of any one of his past successes? And if yesterday's future were to be the same tomorrow, would we not find ourselves sacri-ficing the present?

Sacrificing the present! Only the very young should be able to view that sacrifice with complacency; and yet how many of us can be sure that we are not prisoners of the future which recedes con-tinuously and never arrives at all . . .

Let there be no doubt about it: man can only thus realise himself in the present. The past is the memory of the present, and the future will cease to be future when it arrives. But let there be no mistake about this: to work for a better tomorrow is one task of the present; to harvest the grain which was planted long ago is another.

Be that as it may, my decision was taken: I would turn the page, and I would be ready to harvest the ripe wheat which stood along my route. This left my family, my children . . . Paradoxically enough, I had less trouble with my conscience over them than over my work. I firmly believe that a father should strive to be a man out of the ordinary, for his children's benefit. They ought to feel proud of him, and proud to bear his name.

From this point of view my voyage was going to offer them a new interest—for the first time we would be writing to each other and enjoying the special insight that letters give. I had never felt myself so close to my children as I did during those years of separa-tion. My wife preferred to stay at home; boats frightened her, and she fancied the role of indulgent parent at home much more than that of a storm-tossed traveller far from port. With an obstinacy typical of the Ardennes (from which she came) she elected to have all the advantages of marriage and none of its inconveniences dur-ing my absence. This resolute decision set my conscience at rest. It was very important to me to be able to set out with nothing on my mind, causing no regret and feeling no remorse. My mother was nearly eighty-five years old; had I the right to make her suffer the pain of such a long separation? That worried me for quite a time; in the end it turned out that she found good cause for satisfaction in my project. Napoleon said: 'The future of the child is the work of the mother', and this was a good augury. My mother was very romantic, and remembered nothing about the sailor's life except his supposed success with women. She did not worry about the dangers of the deep, and wished me happy landings rather than epic achievements at sea.

Since I first began to learn about navigation I had always taken every chance of improving my knowledge. My first whale-boat had been replaced by a better one, and then by a small trawler, the Z485 *Antoinette*, registered at the port of Zeebrugge. I went out in her regularly, summer and winter, and I had learnt quite a lot about coastal navigation. I gave myself regular practice in the use of the sextant. On holidays I was often to be seen at the end of the mole at Zeebrugge or at the end of the jetty at Blankenberge shooting the sun towards the end of the afternoon, when it is low above the sea. The technique of navigation fascinated me, and I quickly mastered all the traditional ways of fixing one's position.

I had also read a great deal during the last few years. From Gerbault to the Van de Wieles, from Slocum to Tilman, I devoured every book I could find, and it was through their adventures that I learnt about the sea. Disregarding for a moment the obviously substantial contribution made by her designer, *Williwaw* largely embodies what I had gleaned from those books, reading between the lines, sometimes deducing the truth from their mistakes, but always taking as my starting point the real experiences of my elders. I know that the proverb says: 'Years are wiser than books', and doubtless I am better informed about the subject now that I have had the opportunity to compare my own experiences with those which came to me from my reading. Books, however, provide an excellent foundation on which to build, which no-one should neglect.

A sailing ship intended to travel in distant regions, where specialised technical assistance is hard to find, must be built of a material which is easy to repair. Steel is a good example of such a material. When you are dealing with a steel hull, most things can be put right with simple welding equipment, or even with a drill and a bagful of rivets. The great strength of the metal and its ability to bend instead of breaking are further important advantages. It cannot of course be denied that sailing ships made of wood, glass fibre, or even cement have proved perfectly satisfactory all over the world. I am sure they will continue to do so as long as they meet with normal conditions. But who can be sure that he will never be involved in a collision, never run aground? One has only to think of running into a submerged log or a sleeping whale, of dragging an anchor, or of hitting a buoy which has come adrift. A thousand dangers lie in wait for the sailor. As Gerard Borg rightly reminds us in one of his books: 'Belt-and-braces never lets you down!'

Someone may object that steel is a heavy material and is only suitable for big vessels; that is true in a way, but it depends on what you want. If the boat is intended for regatta sailing, extra weight is a much more serious disadvantage than a relative lack of strength. What matters above all, in this case, is winning races, even if this means the occasional accident or a reduction in the life of the boat.

On the other hand, if the boat is intended for long and ambitious voyages, the objective is quite different: endurance becomes the most important factor. Once sailing has ceased to be a summer hobby, and becomes a basis of a new existence, the idea of safety takes on a totally new importance—so does the idea of comfort— and a new way of life emerges.

To my mind, the light-weight boat is not really suitable for long journeys. Its lack of stability and jerky movement make it a tiring companion; its fragility may sometimes make it a dangerous one. I have never regretted the size or the weight of my *Williwaw*; she has, in fact, exceeded my expectations, and even my hopes.

I mentioned comfort a moment ago, and I should like to say something further on the subject. At sea comfort is a necessity, in that it contributes to improved safety. A comfortable bunk, which allows you to sleep well, is necessary because it increases your physical resources. The same is true of the automatic pilot, the echo-sounder, the well equipped galley and various other devices which will help you to be a better sailor—but I must again insist on the fact that comfort should be a means to the end of improved safety. The pursuit of convenience for its own sake can have negative results. Thus a heater, which can be very useful, becomes a

23

disadvantage if it keeps you below when your presence is needed on deck. A small generator can be a great help, but if there is nowhere suitable on board to keep the petrol which it requires, you are better off without it.

Among the gadgets which are to be found on the market, some are useful, some are completely useless, and some potentially useful in certain circumstances. A choice has to be made, in the light of one's own aptitudes and those of one's crew, when one is fitting out one's boat. The special knowledge of an electronics engineer, for example, could justify his purchase of a piece of equipment which it would be unwise to recommend to anyone else. The ideal boat must be a function of the personality of its crew and of the voyage which it is going to undertake as well as of the plan of its designer.

Williwaw was designed by L. Van de Wiele as an 18-ton steel ketch measuring 13 metres LOA, with a 3.8-metre beam and a 1.9-metre draft. She was powered by a Thornycroft 4-cylinder Diesel engine giving about 62 HP at 2250 r.p.m. Self-steering was provided by Decca Electronic Pilot.

Perhaps this is a good moment to say a few words about the sort of voyage for which *Williwaw* was intended. Anyone who plans to make an important journey by sea begins by establishing his destination, and then goes on to review the different routes which are available in order to select the one which best suits his boat and his crew. If one is planning a circumnavigation of the world from east to west, one can reach the Pacific Ocean either by the Caribbean Sea and the Panama Canal, or by rounding the southern tip of South America (round the Horn or through the Straits of Magellan or the Beagle Channel; or again by forcing the North-West Passage via the Arctic Ocean and the Bering Strait). Personally, I felt attracted by the Cape Horn route. There was no special glory attached to this choice; but, as I mentioned before, I wanted to feel myself in a state of total responsibility—which implies total activity —during this journey. Total activity is very hard to achieve in the conditions which generally prevail in equatorial regions, where the temperature encourages repose rather than action.

The North-West Passage had been made famous by the expedition of Amundsen in 1906. He was the first to make his way from the Atlantic through to the Bering Strait and the open waters of the

Pacific. But I was not ready at that time to undertake such a difficult voyage.

The southern route—which looked very promising when I studied the charts of Tierra del Fuego and Patagonia—seemed to fit in best with my basic requirements. As soon as I had taken the decision, I began a serious study of the route. Not long afterwards I set sail and began my voyage round the world.

3

Circumnavigation and Self-Discovery

My object is not to describe my journey around the world, but my successful completion of the North-West Passage. But the one cannot be wholly dissociated from the other. My business career, my circumnavigation and my Arctic voyage are all separate chapters of the same existence. As I said before, '*Man can only realise himself in the present.*' As a man advances through life, all the moments through which he has lived are ineluctably added to his character, modelling it, adapting it, or transforming it, sometimes for the better sometimes for the worse, according to circumstances. To improve my chances of being understood, I must say a few words about my voyage round the world. I was alone for much of this journey, and it confronted me with myself more completely than anything had done before. This experience had a profound effect on me.

We are all aware that our personality is modelled by influences of different, sometimes opposing, kinds. These influences generally express themselves for me by an interior dialogue between voices. One sets the targets, feeling its way towards an ideal capable of satisfying its intelligence and its humanity. The second represents the executive function, on which the first relies to have its ideas carried out and to which it prescribes an appropriate course of action. I am very surprised to have found no mention of the importance of this interior dialogue in the writings of other solitary navigators. I conclude that most people do not like to admit that they talk to themselves. For my part, I have no hesitation in admitting that I talk to myself regularly, and I shall often make use of this dialogue to weigh my aspirations against my ability to achieve them at each stage. In any case, I do not believe that a solitary traveller can endure his condition for long without this method of interior self-expression. Far from being a burden, solitude has been an extremely enriching experience for me, once I could bring my two voices into harmony.

This harmony reveals itself as an inward peace, which is the first step towards happiness. Various conditions are necessary if we are to reach this stage. On the one hand, we must not demand from ourselves more than we can give. Each personality has a number of innate and unchangeable characteristics; if a man with no musical ear tries to force himself to become a Rubinstein he will saddle himself with an internal conflict that can have no outcome. On the other hand, the executive function must always be ready to do what it is told, and must learn to will what it has to do. It must, furthermore, compel itself to ignore the promptings of instinct and obey those of reason.

A perfect balance must be achieved between one's aspirations and one's abilities; and this presupposes a profound knowledge of oneself. Solitude compels us to face what we have to do alone, and thus gives us a unique opportunity to draw up a personal balance-sheet. We clearly can and must improve ourselves as we go along, for neither our desires nor our abilities are always the same. This implies that our internal harmony must be constantly readjusted; inward peace is not something that one can acquire once and for all.

My perception of these and other psychological mechanisms was of great help to me in attaining the state of mental preparation required to face my northern voyage in a reasonable manner. I must emphasise that the necessary technical preparation, made up of many interlocking factors, is completed when one is on one's own, dealing with the specific difficulties that arise during the voyage. The solitary traveller can expect no direct help from any-body, and every problem that arises must be dealt with by him, alone and from his own resources. Thus his behaviour in the face of the complex mass of difficulties which beset him is intimately linked with his internal peace and his confidence in himself.

Sailing in company with others is less instructive from the point of view of one's own abilities, but it introduces a new set of hazards in terms of individual relations, especially on board a small vessel. A man of well-balanced character, who is at peace with himself (and therefore has no complexes), will however undoubtedly have an easy relationship with other people. A spell of solitude, if it does in fact lead to internal peace, will subsequently enable a man to achieve better relations in a group. Solitude in the strict sense can have a very different effect on different individuals. Personally, I feel it only in physical matters—in having only one pair of arms to hoist a sail, for example. The mental side of solitude has little effect on me. At sea, I never feel alone; I live with my surroundings and in my surroundings. The world is my home, and my memory makes a universe out of it.

It is perhaps time to say a few words about my relation to Nature. Life at sea exposes a man completely to the elements. Simple logic, not to mention the instinct of self-preservation, quickly brought me to a realisation of their power. Only a fool would think that he could measure his own strength against them. I do not throw down a challenge to Cape Horn, I do not defy the sea or its dangers. On the contrary I try to avoid those dangers. I have far more faith in human intelligence than in human muscle. Man may be the cleverest of all animals but he is far from being the strongest; a bear, a whale or an elephant is incomparably more powerful. But human knowledge is part of human development, and improves with each generation. There is no such growth in physical strength.

All in all, I have a great respect for Nature and regard myself as just one of her children. But that does not prevent me from defending myself—nor from saluting Cape Horn as I sail by. Conscious of the puniness of my strength compared with the power of the elements, I regard the anxiety which I feel when a gale is blowing as the logical consequence of this difference of scale. And so I do not reproach myself for being afraid—on the contrary! I reflect that my perception of danger is working well, which is reassuring. There is no internal conflict, and so I remain completely master of myself, and humble at the same time. It should be noted that self-mastery and humility naturally go together. This is not always apparent!

Towards the end of my voyage round the world, when I left Cape Town and re-entered the waters of the Atlantic, I was suddenly confronted with the prospect of returning home. I felt that the world was very small, and that I would have liked to go a little further. But I had allowed myself three years to 'loop the loop', and only a few months of that period were left. And so I accepted the fact, which seemed quite reasonable, that I would soon have to lay up my boat for quite a long period and look for another job ashore. The return to organised society gave me an unexpected but profound shock. I will explain this later. I sincerely wanted to get back into life on shore, but I nevertheless soon made up my mind to set out on another journey. I had already had thoughts—rather vague ones—of attempting the North-West Passage. I now began to think seriously about it, and began the necessary studies at once.

Arctic navigation is a special subject, and poses many difficult problems. But research into specific difficulties and their solutions soon gave me confidence. I decided to modify *Williwaw* for a journey through the pack-ice. The boat was already in the yard at Thuin, and I had only to say the word for work to begin.

Lending a hand at the yard by day, studying by night and sleeping when I could, I completed the modification and fitting out of the boat and the study of the charts in a little under two years. There had been a considerable rise in costs, which had taken me by surprise. It had also, no doubt, made the owners of the yard extremely gloomy about the future. Despite the publicity which they could expect to gain from the voyage, they were inflexible on the subject of their bill.

Be that as it may, I uttered a deep sigh of relief as I steered *Williwaw* down the Sambre towards the open sea. The early mist cast a grey veil over the slag-heaps and factory chimneys of the district of Charleroi. In the diffused light of the March morning, the gloomy landscape of the 'black country' fled away behind like a nightmare at the dawn of a new day.

Belgian television, well-known for its almost exclusive devotion to cycle racing and soccer, had unexpectedly sent a team on board. Avoiding the expense of a trip out to sea, the R.T.B. contented itself with the background provided by an inland waterway. The masts were still flat on the deck, and to avoid showing them in that position the camera-man concentrated on overhead and low-angle shots which formed a scanty basis for a programme which should have evoked the poetry of sail, pack-ice and the wide open spaces. The television team were a charming and resourceful lot of people; they exploited the contrast between the present scene, which they photographed, and the future voyage which they described most eloquently in words.

The present scene had little to recommend it. After a journey of a couple of hours, my fresh paint was already filthy with the oil lightheartedly discharged into the waters of the canal by the people who live on its banks. No need to worry about that, though—clean water was not far away, and soon afterwards I was out at sea, accompanied by the Flemish television, which had been smarter or more patient than its French-speaking opposite number. By the middle of May, after putting in at various ports to complete my equipment, I had reached Falmouth, my last European port of call before leaving for the far north.

4

A Difficult Departure

Up to this moment the spring of 1977 has not been very agreeable. Easterly gales, which are unusual in the English Channel in May, have blown continuously; and, though that means that we have the wind behind us, Albert and I have been thoroughly soaked on our way to Falmouth. Albert is an excellent sailor, who has come to spend a few weeks on board *Williwaw*, and did intend to come with me all the way to Greenland. But now we are slightly behind schedule, and he is afraid of missing his son's wedding, so he is planning to go back home today. I do not altogether agree with him, and think that *Williwaw* could still get us to Greenland in time for him to keep his engagement. But there is nothing to be done; I cannot convince him. Having argued ourselves out, we bet a good bottle of wine on our respective opinions.

I feel rather sad as I accompany Albert to the station. He has made an excellent crew, blessed with a willing nature. His presence and his help have been very valuable to me, for, I must admit it, I am already very tired at this early stage of the voyage. Dealings with press, radio and television, the tension which inevitably accompanies the last few weeks before sailing, and farewells to family and friends have all combined to take their toll, and I do not feel in the best of form as I finally hoist the sail on this morning of May 21. Fortunately the weather is calm, with a gentle breeze to help me on my way. Towards evening I round the Land's End lighthouse, and during the night I see another lighthouse on the Scilly islands wink a final farewell from Europe.

My first day of solitude has allowed me to organise my ideas; these last twenty-four hours have also abruptly brought me face to face with reality. In the past few months, I have so often been asked about navigation in the Arctic and have repeated all the details so many times that I have reached the stage of being able to say my piece by heart, quite confident that no-one would catch me out: I knew all the answers, and everything seemed fine. But now that my attempt on the North-West Passage is really under way, I begin to wonder whether all that may not be a bit of a mirage. Is reality going to confirm my theories, or am I shortly going to discover that they are nothing but a series of elaborate guesses? The technical literature about navigation in the far north has not, in general, been much worked over. I have often learned of problems only by a process of deduction; and my answers to those problems may well seem somewhat chancy. This belated lack of confidence is tiresome, not to say maddening; for if conditions do turn out differently from my expectations, I shall still have a head on my shoulders, and shall no doubt be able to correct my aim and adapt my ideas to circumstances. And anyway, when you have set your hand to the plough, you must not look back! My choice is a simple one: either I take the risk of going ahead on the basis of the knowledge I have gathered, or I refuse to take it—in which case there's nothing for me to do but to turn round, go home and humbly confess that I have made a mistake.

These thoughts occupy me during the day, but half an hour after midnight the B.B.C. announces further strong winds from the east for the next twenty-four hours. The prospect of dirty weather is a welcome diversion. I must prepare for the blast as soon as possible. I find that I do not after all feel strongly enough about things to want to turn and beat back against the wind; and so I prudently continue on my westerly course.

The wind grows gradually stronger during the night, and I lower the mizzen-sail. At about 0700 I judge that it is time to take in some reefs in the mainsail. I lower the boom slightly by slacking off the halyard, and am irritated to see that the winch-handle strikes against the guard-rail recently placed around the mast, preventing me from turning the boom. As the sail has meanwhile begun to flog furiously, I put the boat head to wind. Finally I am compelled to lower the sail.

I ought to have tested the furling gear before setting out! Reproaching myself for my mistake, I decide (partly to punish myself) to set the trysail—a job which takes me some time! This manoeuvre is simple enough in theory, but less so in practice, with a wind blowing. You have to take just as many precautions to ensure that you stay on board yourself as to prevent the sail from catching the wind and beginning to flap while you are threading the blocks on to the rail. But I organise the manoeuvre very thoroughly before carrying it out, so that everything follows its logical sequence, and the sail goes up without too much trouble.

I am thoroughly drenched by the spray which the wind drives horizontally across the sea, and some water has gone down the neck of my oilskins. I go below to change, and as I do so I reflect that the hoisting of the trysail was well carried out, and that taking everything into account (including the fact that I have been on my feet ever since I left port), I have not done too badly. This makes me feel better, and helps me to regain my inward harmony. But I still have work to do. Now that the boat is safe with reduced sail, I decide to cook myself a hot meal. I want something elaborate and good. I still have a little fresh meat on board, and decide that an entrecôte 'marchand de vin' with a purée of potatoes would be just the thing. During the preparation of the dish, I carefully put the saucepan containing the decoction of shallots, with its dash of red wine, on top of a wet cloth; but the boat rolls violently, and it flies across the cabin and crashes against the bulkhead.

I quickly repress the obscenity which comes spontaneously to my lips, telling myself that it is better not to get angry, but to take these setbacks with calm—with a smile in fact, if they are as trivial as this one. After washing the cabin sole, I again begin to cut up a bunch of shallots. When the dish is finally ready, the entrecôte and the purée are so thoroughly cooked that I have to change the menu. The new and ironical wording is: 'boeuf bourguignon, pommes duchesse'! But nothing is easy today, and the feast is complicated by the necessity of simultaneously keeping food on plate, plate on table, cutlery within reach, drink in glass and myself on my chair. The most dangerous thing is letting go of everything else in order to cut the meat. But there is nothing like action for restoring one's morale. To combine elaborate cookery with navigating a ship in heavy weather is not easy; but by imposing this difficult task on myself, I gain an opportunity of judging my performance in adverse conditions and of recovering that interior confidence which is indispensable for the future.

As already mentioned, I have not had a chance to sleep since I left Falmouth, and I have now been on my feet for thirty hours. Fatigue begins to hit me hard. This spell of rough weather does not help and adds a considerable amount of extra physical effort to my mental exhaustion. Luckily, the density of the traffic seems to have lessened a little, and it is some time since I last sighted another vessel.

Williwaw is now running well, at an angle of 25° to the following wind on the starboard tack. She is moving as steadily as possible, in view of the present state of the sea, and the risk of gybing seems to me to be small. I might as well take the opportunity and allow myself some rest. I have a signal detector, an inexpensive little device which rings an alarm when its mini-antenna picks up the waves of any radar whatever. This will wake me up if another vessel approaches us; otherwise my alarm clock will wake me up in two hours time so that I can review the situation.

Snugly stowed in my bunk, I have no need of rocking to sleep. But before I drop off I run over the more important events of the day in my mind, as is my habit. I am pleased to have been able to keep awake and alert, for I consider that adherence to the rules is not only an essential condition for safety, but also a moral obligation towards the whole yachting community.

We know that shipping companies and their insurers got very excited at the time of the last single-handed transatlantic race, when they realised that boats as big as *Club Méditerranée* are capable of causing serious damage to their own merchant ships. Since then there has been a strong current of opinion among official bodies in favour of a straightforward ban on single-handed sailing. For all those who, like myself, love to find total freedom at sea, it is now extremely important to be even more careful than before, to avoid playing into the hands of the opposition. The law of the sea is in a state of flux. The sea itself, which was always defined as belonging to nobody, is now claimed by everybody. This makes it all too probable that navigation will become subject to more and more regulations. What a pity! As far as the single-handed transatlantic race is concerned, it must be admitted, I think, that the organisers were ill advised in permitting these very big vessels, which can have adverse effects on yachting as a whole. Besides, it has been widely known for a very long time that a boat's speed is closely connected with its waterline length. To increase the size of a boat with the sole object of making it faster is therefore merely taking the easy way out. It is not a very practical way, either, for what really distinguishes a single-hander's yacht from any other is not so much how well she handles as how easily she can be maintained. From this point of view a very large yacht is certainly not suited to the abilities of a single man, and therefore has no place in a race specifically intended for single-handed sailing.

Suddenly the alarm clock wakes me up, and though I am quite convinced that I have not completely lost consciousness, I have really been asleep; my swollen eyes bear witness to the fact, and the empty feeling in my head confirms it. It must be about 4 in the afternoon and a feeble ray of sunshine can just be detected behind the curtain of the porthole on the port side. The wind does not seem to have dropped, and I can clearly hear the hiss of water under the forefoot.

The movement of the boat helps me up. As I sit on the bunk, one foot automatically reaches out to the sail-bag opposite in search of support, wedging my behind against the side of the bunk so that my arms are free to pull a sweater over my head.

As I get dressed, the following dialogue is to be heard:

'What filthy weather, damn it! I hope to God that there are no ships in sight and that I can have a bit more sleep before I have to cook my supper!'

'Put your oilskins on, Willy! There's no point in getting wet and having to put a lot of stuff soaked in sea water with the dirty linen . . . Get moving, now! Get your head outside into the weather!'

As soon as the hatch is open, a noisy, cold, damp wind whips across my face.

'A good thing it's still blowing from the east!'

'You can say that again!'

The horizon is perfectly empty, and everything seems in order on deck. The dinghy, securely lashed, is still there, and the sails, solidly filled, are driving the boat beautifully; a glance at the compass confirms that we are on course.

I want to get below again at once, but just as I am shutting the hatch I notice a bird clutching on to the stern rail. Its feathers are fluffed out to protect it from the cold, and I can see that it has got its metabolism turned well down.

Poor storm-tossed creature, he's not on a very good wicket . . . All things considered, his position is not unlike mine; both of us are physically dominated by our surroundings. He hangs on to the rail, and I hang on to the boat. Each of us tries to adjust himself

35

to exterior conditions, with the equipment that nature has given him.

Deep in thought, I stay and watch him for a moment. From time to time, when the force of the wind or the movement of the boat threatens his precarious equilibrium, he wakes up for a few seconds, pulls his feathers closer about him to lessen his resistance to the wind, lifts his head slightly and half opens his eyes, revealing only the whites; but a moment later his eyes close again, and his head sinks back out of sight among his feathers, which are fluffed out as before. The gusts must go straight through his fragile defences, and from time to time he shudders convulsively.

I can just make out that it's a pigeon. There is a ring round one of his feet.

'Hello, pigeon! . . . Hello, my lad! It must be a bit rough out there!'

No reaction. Not that I expected an answer; but there might have been some sign that he had heard me.

'He must be all in . . . Everyone is all in, on board this boat; and the best thing to do is to follow his example and go to sleep. If he's still there tomorrow, I shall probably be able to give him some-thing to eat and drink; if I approach him now, before he has got used to life on board, I may drive him away.'

After a final look round the horizon, I shut the hatch, set the alarm, and go back to sleep for another two hours.

My rest is much shorter than that, however; I have scarcely dropped off when the signal detector gets me out of my bunk again. When I get on deck, I see several ships, and I have to keep watch for quite a long time. In the evening it seems to me that the wind is dropping. At about 2030 the sun goes down in a clear sky, and a little later, after supper, I hoist the mizzen-sail. The trysail can stay up for the night, during which I shall be getting up a few times to have a look round. And in fact, when morning comes, I have only had a couple of hours sleep, but I feel fine all the same, and decide, as dawn is breaking, to hoist the mainsail again; inward peace is gradually restored, and I am quite happy about the way I have dealt with my initial difficulties.

The pigeon is still there, and I have put a mug of water down for him. Dirty marks on the deck indicate clearly that he is suffering from an intestinal infection, which seems bound to dehydrate him very quickly. So my morning radio call to my friend Guy, who is a doctor, very soon turns into a consultation, and as soon as we have finished our talk I begin looking for the medicine to cure my passenger. Not knowing much about pigeons, I wonder what I ought to give him to eat. I know, of course, that pigeons eat grain; but although I have plenty of food on board, I am not myself graminivorous, and I have not stocked up with maize.

For what it's worth, I boil up some rice, crush some hazel and brazil nuts, break some bread, and put the lot in a bowl, sprinkled with an antibiotic. The bird quickly shows an irresistible passion for nuts. After a few tentative, distrustful pecks, its beak digs into the bowl like a pneumatic drill, searching for nuts and nothing else. The bread and rice are firmly discarded and splashed all over the place . . . It is also quite clear that the medicine has not had any effect as yet.

'Watch it, pigeon! You're tossing it all over the place . . . Just look at you! . . . And what about my paint work? As if you cared! He's going to be a handful, the brute!'

5

Companionship in the Solitude
of the North Atlantic

It is May 23, and when I take my noon sight, I find that the three of us—*Williwaw*, the pigeon and I—are at 50° 24' N., 12° 01' W., which puts us 110 miles south-west of Ireland. 270 miles of the journey have been completed in these first two days at sea. The weather is better, and the sea has lost its violence. Sailing has become a pleasure again, and after putting away the sextant and logging the position I also record the weather conditions: wind north-east, force 4 to 5, barometer 1028 millibars, dropping slowly, clear sky, good visibility, temperature below deck 61°F. The boat is moving well, at about 6 knots, and the alternator operated by the propeller shaft is charging at between 10 and 20 amperes. No difficulty in keeping the batteries charged. This is an important matter, for our consumption of current is relatively high. The automatic pilot has to be supplied with electricity twenty-four hours a day, the radio equipment is also regularly in service, and so is the radar, which I use from time to time when the echo detector reports the presence of a ship which I cannot immediately see. At night, *Williwaw*'s powerful navigation lights add to the general consumption, which would soon run the batteries down if I could not rely on this invaluable charger, which the propeller begins to turn as soon as the boat gets under way, even at a very modest speed. At 4 knots, for example, the charge runs at about 8 amperes; at 5 knots it runs at better than 12 amperes, and it reaches 30 amperes at 8 knots. As our voltage is 24 volts, we can estimate the yield of the alternator as going up to 720 watts, which is ample to supply all our needs. I said just now that the radio equipment is regularly in service; and I am in fact one of the many members of the happy band of radio hams. To have a transmitter on board is to have a friendly porthole open on the whole world. One may enjoy solitude and want no-one else on board—but who would choose to cut himself off from the warmth of a friendly word, from a kindness which comes straight from the heart, a kindness so disinterested that it can truly be called fraternal?

But I can already hear voices raised to tell me that you cannot truly enter into communion with the spirit of the deep if you simultaneously keep up a dialogue with the land. It is true that most of us love the pure simplicity of life which we see in the great kingdom of Nature, and hope to find it at sea. But I do not see how one can truly love Nature if one does not also stay in communication with mankind. (I am not speaking of human society, but of human individuals.) It is all very well to wonder at the flight of the albatross; if we do not also appreciate the miracle of human intelligence, something must be wrong.

There can also be no doubt that in the conditions of isolation and danger inherent in arctic navigation, a good radio link is desirable for safety, and considerably increases one's chances of survival in the event of a serious mishap.

There is always someone waiting to take a message on the ham wavebands, and any call for help will not only be picked up, but will immediately find a multitude of operators willing and able to relay the message to the rescue services. I am convinced that, in remote areas where there is little traffic at sea, the hams often provide a better service than the professional network—and that alone is enough to justify the installation of a transmitter. To operate a ham station a licence is necessary; the examination is not very easy, and considerable effort is necessary to pass it. In my view this is a very good thing, for it means that the candidate must be really competent and really motivated. These two qualities form an indispensable combination if the quality of radio communications is to be maintained.

The basic object of the radio ham is to acquire, by a process of trial and error, a thorough knowledge of the electronic phenomena and the laws which govern communication by Hertzian waves. Nearly 800,000 hams cover the whole world, and the modern S.S.B. transmitter makes it possible for any one of them to contact any other in normal conditions, even if he is on the other side of the world.

The justification for these contacts traditionally lies in the exchange of technical information; and many hams have undoubtedly a passionate interest in electronics. It is generally through these technical discussions, which serve as a sort of universal language, that other matters of common interest are discovered. Through these contacts, you may find to your surprise that the thinking of a Patagonian fisherman corresponds exactly to your own, and that a little artisan in Singapore uses exactly the same friendly expressions to you as a bank clerk in Bogota or your friend Claude in Toulouse.

You may sometimes be especially enchanted by a conversation because of the fellow-feeling which you can detect in the mere words of an unknown contact, of whom you have no clear mental picture. Cheerful smile or inexpressive mask, Hercules or midget . . . What does it matter! At these starry moments, only the language of the heart is important. We quite naturally get in touch again, and before long the technical side is forgotten and we find ourselves getting into contact with each other as old friends. This has happened to me on numerous occasions, and I shall never forget, among other examples, my contacts with Albert (FR7AK) to whom I used to speak every morning. He was transmitting from the island of Reunion and I was sailing in the Indian Ocean at the time. We hit it off from our very first contact, and I enjoyed all our subsequent conversations. He sang the praises of his island home, and I told him all about my boat. The day came when I accepted an invitation from him and stopped off at Reunion. He was there to shake my hand even before I had tied up.

On May 27, at the end of my first week at sea, I am at 51° 59' N., 22° 07' W., or about 700 miles from Falmouth, well on the way towards Greenland. My route is turning out very well: I started by sailing mainly west but heading slightly north, to avoid both the traffic which converges towards the English Channel and that which rounds the south of Ireland. Later, I avoided any further northing before I reached 30° W., so as not to run into cold and fog before I had had a chance to catch up with my sleep. The depression is moving in the opposite direction, to the east, taking the cloud and drizzle with it. The barometer is at 1022 millibars, rising slowly, and the sun is coming through again.

I feel less worried: life on board has gradually organised itself, and I feel the satisfaction of having got on top of things again. The pigeon, too, has got over his illness and is gaining strength. He is a bird of uncertain temper, and apt to dispute possession of what he thinks of as his pigeon loft, though I persist in regarding it as my boat! From time to time the fancy takes him to leave his perch and circle round the boat a couple of times; but there is always a group of sea-birds gliding over our wake, and they soon begin to chase him. He swoops back on to his perch, safe from his pursuers and pleased to have got his form back.

I must admit that the pigeon gives me a hell of a lot of work. He is a greedy bird, hungry all the time—and what goes in must come out! I'm always mopping up after him. Though I make a special attempt to protect my charts, he has already added several groups of islands to the one of the North Atlantic. But I haven't the heart to chase him away. He is no match for the birds of prey, and the thought of losing him is more than I can bear. I shall have to put up with him, though he is an infernal nuisance, and I shall do all I can to help him to stay alive—he has plenty to contend with already.

Taking advantage of the calmer weather this afternoon, I decide to open up a box of 16 mm film, so that my camera will be ready for immediate use. I had had some difficulty at Falmouth in finding the right type of film for my cassette cameras, which have the advantage that you can load them easily even when wearing heavy gloves. The firm did not have the cassettes in stock, and had to order them specially from the factory.

I had to delay my departure by several days, and I remember that Albert and I had been afraid that we would have to wait for several weeks. But fortunately it was not all that long before we received a telephone message to say that the cassettes had arrived, and that we could pick them up at our convenience. Delighted by our good luck, we immediately hailed a taxi, and it was not long before the three boxes of one hundred cassettes each were on board. They were well packed, and we had plenty of cassettes left over from those I had bought in Belgium to cover our immediate requirements, so we packed the boxes away without opening them, thinking that it would be time enough to open them when we needed them. In the past week, however, I had used up the remaining Belgian cassettes, so the moment had now arrived. I had some difficulty in cutting the metal bands which secured the box, but managed it in a couple of minutes, only to discover, to my horror, that it contained rolls of film instead of cassettes.

Damn it! Damn it! Damn it! . . . I immediately check the contents of the other boxes. They are all the same! This is a real catastrophe; I cannot do without the right kind of film. My first thought is to call up my friend Guy on the radio, so that he can get in touch with the responsible firm. But then I reflect that it is Friday, and already too late to get anything useful done before Monday. For the moment I don't know whether to go on to Greenland or turn back to England. To go on without the films may be to lose an important record of my voyage in the far north. To turn back means losing at least three weeks, which is not a very attractive prospect. But I must be in a position to recover part of the money I have invested in this expedition at a later stage, and the film is essential for this. I have no choice; and, sick at heart, I decide to turn back.

It is 1825, on Friday May 27. Having already completed 720 miles on the way to Greenland, I set a course of 107°, towards the mouth of the English Channel.

Lucky pigeon, you're going home! That is my only consolation; otherwise the picture is pretty black. I don't like the idea of getting back into a busy shipping lane. I must have some rest before going on watch again, and I realise that it is not just a matter of getting back to England. I shall then have to set out again, as quickly as possible so as to limit the delay to the minimum. Whatever happens, I am not prepared to continue the journey and find myself penniless at the end of it. I value my self-sufficiency, and I know that the price of personal liberty is to maintain one's financial independence. We live in a world where money is indispensable. The fact has to be admitted—and I have no wish to be a beggar!

Foreseeing an exhausting time to come, I go to bed early. There is little wind, and progress is slow. Guy has gone off for the weekend and I do not expect to be able to contact him before Monday morning. Tomorrow I shall try to get in touch with another Belgian station, which may be able to contact Guy by telephone at Nieuport, where he is spending two days on board his boat *Procax*, and explain the situation to him, so that the necessary steps can be taken as early as possible on Monday. There is no time to lose. The cassettes *must* be ready when I arrive. I have a disturbed night. I fully realise that I may be losing the opportunity of completing the first stage of the voyage this year. I am not a rich man, and I have invested a large part of my capital in this project. Since every day that passes involves expenditure and since a large part of my stores have a limited shelf-life, a twelve-month delay would involve a considerable financial loss. The sum involved is in fact probably greater than the one I stand to lose through not being able to take any film—and that is a loss which would itself compromise my future.

In other words, if I miss this year, there is nothing for me to do but admit that I have made a big mistake and regret the loss of my personal liberty. I'm not being sorry for myself; I am merely facing the facts. If my North-West Passage robs me of my self-sufficiency, it will be a setback. I may get over it, but it will still have been a setback.

Today, Saturday, I have managed to get in contact with ON7FF of Ypres, in the morning. He has telephoned Nieuport Yacht Club, but without result—Guy is not to be found. I can't do anything more for the moment; I've got to wait.

The weather is as undecided as I am. There is no wind at all, and a thick mist envelops the boat, which makes virtually no headway—just as I myself am making no headway towards a solution of my problem.

On Sunday morning, at about 1115 I receive a call from Noël (ON6FN), who assures me that there is no difficulty about sending parcels to Greenland, and that there are several flights daily between Denmark and Greenland. Noël will personally get in contact with England to find out if they are ready to send my cassettes to Greenland, and he will give me the answer tomorrow, Monday, at 11 o'clock. In fact I have full confidence in the good faith of the British firm; I am quite sure that they will be as distressed as I am myself when they find out about their mistake. If the connection with Greenland is available, they will do all they can to send me the cassettes but it all seems too good to be true. Anyway, I decide to heave-to, and not to take any further steps until I have more information.

Sunday wears on. Deeply concerned by my situation, I am fully aware of one thing: for me, doubts about my ability to cope bring a special danger with them. The fear of failure will inevitably increase my fatigue, and fatigue in its turn will increase the stress from which I am suffering, and will take me down into a depressive spiral. So I must not lose confidence; I must contrive to see my difficulties in a less critical and less disastrous light; I must convince myself that I am capable of effective resistance to fatigue. To sum up, I must give myself a course of treatment.

I take a little time out to think what would be best for me. My conclusions are as follows: I must attach due importance to food, and eat well and regularly; I must try to alternate mental and physical effort; I must avoid all waste of energy; I must choose a comfortable point of sailing and avoid carrying too much sail, etc.; I must also avoid worry by keeping busy. I must try to sleep whenever possible and look after my own comfort and wellbeing.

In his book *Ice Bird*, David Lewis, who is a doctor, gives a list of medicines which can delay the onset of fatigue. No doubt they have their value in ordeals of relatively short duration, but to my mind they are dangerous in situations where one cannot give one's body the rest it requires within a reasonable time. So I do not plan to mask the effects of fatigue, but rather to reduce its causes. I shall not drink any more coffee or tea, to avoid deceiving myself about my real condition. I have the satisfaction of having looked my problems in the face, and I feel calmer now. My confidence has come back, and I am sure that my resources, with the help of common sense, will be enough to get me out of difficulty. At least, I have faith that this will be so. But in fact I am not after all to be confronted with this particular test, for this morning Noël tells me that Kodak in the United States will send the cassettes to Egedesminde in Greenland, and that I shall be able to take delivery of them on arrival.

There is no need to describe the joy which this news gives me. I put the boat back on course at once. Hooray! On with the voyage! Thank you, brother hams!

After a short rest, I clean up the cabin and tidy everything. Then I take a bath (in a bucket) and change all my clothes. I love the sensation of clean clothes on a clean skin. I feel a lot better!

6

The Approach to Greenland

On June 1, the noon sight puts us in 54° 48' N., 29° 13' W., or just over 1000 miles from Falmouth. This is a relatively good position, though a little too far north for my liking. Cape Farewell, the most southerly point of Greenland, is 560 miles away on a true bearing of 302°; but the Pilot Chart for the month of June indicates that the cape is still icebound—and there is a real risk of running into icebergs to the north of latitude 56°. My margin of safety accordingly is very limited.

I have kept my resolution to pay special attention to my cooking. My morale is definitely better, but I wish I could sleep longer. My companion, the pigeon, who has been christened 'Mathurin' by my fellow hams, has taken up permanent residence on board. I have fixed up a perch for him in the rear cabin, and I have got used to the idea of having to clear up his nightly mess every morning. The perch is a short length of broom-handle, attached to a shelf with sticky paper. It is getting colder now, and my companion does not wait for an invitation to come inside at nightfall. He obviously enjoys the comfort provided by this improvised perch. I have made a note of the number on his ring, and I have asked Noël to trace the owner and tell him that his pigeon has booked a passage on an Atlantic cruise. The bird's health is excellent now; his temper is as uncertain as ever, but I put up with it in a friendly spirit. He gives me the opportunity to do my daily good deed. One unfortunate point is that my supply of nuts is going down, and I do not know if I shall be able to find any more.

Shortly before midday on June 3, we sail into thick mist—I say we, because I always feel that I am sharing my journey with the boat—and when I take my noon observation, I have to guess the level of the horizon. In these circumstances, I naturally prefer to trust to dead reckoning which places us in 55° 47' N., 33° 05' W. The wind rises rapidly from force 5 to force 6 and then to force 7. Strange to say, the fog does not disperse and remains extremely dense, visibility being practically nil. I have lowered the mainsail

45

and am under headsails and mizzen which enables me to sail closer to the wind. I am now theoretically in the iceberg belt. I should really prefer a less northerly route, and I have been thinking about it for several days; but the wind has been astonishingly constant in direction and has not allowed me to set a more suitable course. I have had to choose between sailing 10° too far to the north or 90° too far to the south. Hoping for a change in wind direction, I have stayed on the more northerly course—quite logically, it seems to me. The radar is operating the whole time, to warn me of any possible icebergs. The fresh breeze carries the boat along at a good speed; evening comes on and soon we are sailing into the night. I stay on watch for a good part of the time, and at 10 o'clock the following morning (Saturday, June 4), weather conditions are as follows: barometer steady at 1030 millibars, wind north-west force 5, temperature 46°F., sky overcast. At 1100 the sun makes a brief appearance and visibility improves. The noon observation indicates that we are running into the danger zone, having now reached 57° 02' N., 35° 45' W.

As visibility is good, I decide to stay on the same course for the rest of the afternoon, and then to turn south, so that I shall be able to sleep with relative peace of mind. The following morning a Norwegian ship (call signal E.L.O.E.E./mm) sends me a warning of imminent strong winds from the west. As I wait for this to materialise, I notice that the breeze has slackened and shortly afterwards it drops completely. Probably the Norwegian's forecast is a little out of date, and really refers to the squall which I have just ridden out. As the hours go by, a long period of still weather sets in; in the evening the boat is completely becalmed, and I am lucky enough to have an excellent night's sleep.

No noon observation on June 6. We are again caught in the fog. Towards the evening a little wind gets up, and I set off towards the south-west.

On the morning of the 7th the boat is again completely becalmed, and we make no progress all day. The sky is grey, the sun is invisible, and there is a persistent mist. At about 10 at night, a breeze at last gets up, and I listen happily to the water running past the hull again. The wind keeps up all through the night, and by the morning we have covered a fair distance. Our estimated position at midday on Tuesday is 56° 45' N., 42° 00' W.

My plan is to reach a point which is still 318 miles away, at 60° N., 50° W., and then to run north along the 50th meridian until we sight the west coast of Greenland. The object is to avoid the heavy seas which are generally to be found off Cape Farewell.

We reach the first turning-point on the morning of June 11, and I am glad to alter due north. We are now approaching the entrance to Davis Strait. Cape Farewell is 185 miles to the east, while on the other side, 435 miles to the west, are the stormy waters of the Labrador Sea and Hudson Strait, with Baffin Island lying a little further to the north.

John Davis, Henry Hudson, William Baffin . . . the earlier stages of the discovery of the north are commemorated by those names. Other men will complete the story, and write the golden book of arctic adventure with their hopes, their successes, and also, alas, their sacrifices.

Early on the afternoon of June 11, as we are making our way into Davis Strait, the wind suddenly freshens. Before long, I have to hand the mainsail and even the jib. The sea gets up, and the wind blows the crests off the waves into white, trailing masses of spume. The marbled sea now reflects a sky traversed by flying clouds, and now sparkles in a fleeting ray of sunshine. Everything is on the move: the whole scene is full of salt spray, of the shriek of the wind, the lament of the rigging. The wind rages everywhere, and there is no shelter except inside my valiant *Williwaw*. Holding on to keep my balance, and maintaining a prudent interval between my nose and the scuttle, I look at the tempest outside from the safety of the cabin. The bow plunges untiringly into each attacking wave, and lifts again as soon as it is passed, slicing off great masses of water which chase across the deck and finally escape through the scuppers as the boat heels beneath the thrust of the swell. I participate in every movement; I feel every vibration; I hear every lament. I lend the boat a part of my life; I endow her with part of my soul. She is more than a mere shell of steel; she is my companion in battle.

Before coming below, I had tried to persuade Mathurin to take shelter. Contrary to my expectations, he did not want to do anything of the kind. His behaviour had an aggressive, obstinate quality, which I well recollect. I put his strange behaviour down to his independence of character, and thought no more about it.

But later an especially violent gust reminded me that he was still outside; so I tried once more to get him to come in, opening the hatch and showing him some nuts to lure him down. But it was a waste of time; he would not come.

During the afternoon the wind slackens. We have made good progress, and Greenland cannot be very far away now—perhaps 60 miles. The boat is going along nicely, and I decide that the time has come to hoist some sail again. Busy on deck, I remember the pigeon. But where is he?

'Hiding, are you, my lad? . . . Where have you got to, you brute?'

A sudden foreboding gives me an unpleasant shock. 'Oh, no! Mathurin! . . .' He's gone; he has answered the call of the land, and I haven't even had the pleasure of seeing him fly away in the right direction. My eyes mist over for a moment, and I make a silent prayer for his future welfare. Will he ever see his native England again?

In the evening we are becalmed once more, so I lower all sail, lash the helm and, after washing up and a good stow, go to sleep. Tomorrow land will be in sight!

7

Some Technical Information

In 1585 John Davis, with forty-one seamen, set sail from England in the three-masted barques *Sunneshine* of 50 tons and *Mooneshine* of 35 tons, fitted out by the merchants of London and the West. His object was to discover a sea route which would make it possible to reach the Indies without interference from the Spanish and Portuguese, who controlled the southern routes. Martin Frobisher had set out on the same quest a few years earlier; and the same motive inspired John Cabot and his son Sebastian to make the voyage which led to the discovery of Newfoundland and Labrador in 1497.

Davis sighted the east coast of Greenland, rounded its most southerly point, which he named Cape Farewell ('Farvel' in Danish) and ran up the west coast of the island, through the waters of the Strait which today bears his name. He was the first to record the existence of this strait, which he explored up to the latitude of 72° 42' N.—a little short of where Upernavik stands today—during his third voyage, in 1587.

John Davis's explorations attracted much attention, and led to the fitting out of several further expeditions. It has been said of Davis that 'he guided Hudson into his Strait and Baffin into his Bay'. Apart from his contribution to geographical discovery, Davis must be regarded as the father of the ship's log book, which is still maintained today in the form which he laid down. He also invented an instrument which was the precursor of the sextant, and published several works on navigation. One of them *The Seaman's Secrets*, was the *vade-mecum* of British sailors for many years.

I quote these achievements of Davis with special pleasure, because we too often think that the sailors of earlier days knew practically nothing, and that the ships of those times were slow old tubs. It cannot be denied that ship-building has since made some progress, or that an auxiliary engine adds greatly to a vessel's manoeuvrability—but I should like to point out that in 1578 (some years before Davis set out), Francis Drake, on board the 90-foot *Golden Hind*, sailed through the Straits of Magellan, from Cape

Virgenes to Cape Pilar, in sixteen days. This record has never been beaten by a vessel propelled only by sail.

Over fifty years earlier, Magellan, on his original voyage of discovery, covered the same course in thirty-seven days, which is a really remarkable performance in the circumstances.

To appreciate this fully, it must be realised that later on, when the great sailing ships were constantly plying round the Horn, the Strait of Magellan was regarded as being virtually impassable, especially from east to west. We know the names of several ships which took more than eighty days to get through. This indicates that the ships of the sixteenth century, far from being 'old tubs' had excellent sea-going qualities, and that their crews were, to say the least, seasoned sailors.

Amundsen and his companions gave proof of an equally remarkable endurance. Nothing could stop the progress of *Gjøa*—neither the pack-ice, nor the hazards of navigation, nor even the continued sufferings strung out by Time. No! I do not underestimate my predecessors. I know how much I owe to their example, and I hope, as the Arctic opens up for me, that I shall be able to match their fortitude.

I include these brief notes because without them some readers might form a false impression regarding the scope of the often dramatic experiences of those who, in centuries gone by, sailed the northern seas in search of a route to the Pacific. Some readers might in fact have regarded a voyage through the waters of the Arctic in 1977 as little more than a pleasure trip—which would really be taking the moon for green cheese.

In point of fact, the world of ice is the enemy of those who do not know it well, and survival itself may become a difficult matter. To tackle the far north without learning all that one can about its specific characteristics would be pure folly. I personally did not feel myself ready to start until I had spent a long time looking for relevant problems and finding solutions to them. This gave me the interior confidence which is indispensable if one is to get through a long period of living right up to the limits of which one is capable. For that is exactly what is involved.

For a man who is used to the comforts of our civilisation, arctic navigation demands a significant physical and mental readjustment. The constant tension produced by the potential dangers posed by the ice and its uncertain movements, the utter loneliness of the far north, and, more generally speaking, the stress which naturally arises from any condition of unaccustomed constraint, can be successfully endured only after a rigorous preparation. As I have already mentioned, my earlier voyages had gone far towards giving me the necessary training, and I was not afraid of solitude. Navigation in the far north, however, still has its special characteristics, and I had to study them, and learn how to adapt myself to them, before I could feel ready to set out.

In the interests of clarity, and to avoid overloading the narrative with technical explanations, I think it will be useful to insert here a brief summary of the principal difficulties to be expected by the navigator in the Arctic.

Continuous Daylight

At the latitudes where we live, the movement of the sun governs the essential rhythm of our lives. The times when we work, sleep and eat are controlled by the alternation of night and day. At the poles, on the other hand, light and darkness divide the whole year between them; there are six months of uninterrupted daylight, and six months of night. Since there is no daily cycle, and consequently no system of natural signals to prompt the traveller to perform his various physiological functions, a visitor to high latitudes has to pay extra attention to the maintenance of an orderly pattern of life. This is a discipline essential to the preservation of his physical and mental faculties.

I know from experience that it takes a lot of willpower to stick to a strict timetable, especially in difficult circumstances. Is there anyone who can say that he has never omitted to cook himself a meal on a day when there were heavy seas running?

In the Arctic, it is not a matter of a few days of difficult conditions, but of weeks or months; and in these circumstances it can be fatal to let oneself go. Obviously, it is not the fact of being late for a meal that is dangerous—nor even the fact of missing a meal altogether, though that is already a more serious matter. The danger is that a failure of discipline will slowly and imperceptibly bring about a loss of physical resistance, and that the resulting weakness will come to light at a critical moment. An exhausted body and a strong will are seldom to be found together. That is the real danger, for in extreme conditions life itself often depends on the will to live.

Since it is extremely difficult, when the sky is overcast, to tell the morning from the afternoon, a chronometer with a twenty-four hour dial is indispensable. So is a watch which indicates the date of the month—though a barograph with a weekly cycle can be used as a substitute if necessary. Dry-cell batteries do not stand up to frost, and so watches which depend on them are not suitable for the Arctic.

Charts

Mercator's projection is very widely used for charts of the oceans, but it cannot cope with the convergence of the meridians towards the poles, and is therefore unsuited to high latitudes. To illustrate this shortcoming, it should be said that a given distance along the equator on a Mercator chart appears to be three times as long at latitude 70°; and the figure would rise to infinity at the poles. The increasing distortion to which areas represented by Mercator's projection are subject, in regions to the north of the 70th parallel, is therefore regarded as wholly inconsistent with the requirements of navigation.

To put it in more practical terms—the rhumb line connecting two points on a Mercator's projection differs so widely from the great circle, or shortest possible route between two points on the surface of the globe, that it cannot be used for planning one's route.

For the same reasons, the calculation of distances becomes more and more complicated as one goes further north. So I had to familiarise myself with Lambert's projection, which is generally used for the regions now under consideration. This is an improved conical projection, which was worked out by a self-taught Alsatian geographer, Jean Lambert (1728–77). A straight line, on Lambert's projection, represents a great circle for all practical purposes. This means that the representation of surfaces remains very accurate, in this projection.

The Compass

The proper functioning of the magnetic compass depends on the horizontal component of terrestrial magnetism. Near the poles, the intensity of this component greatly decreases, and the vertical directivity, which is no use for a compass, becomes predominant. It is generally reckoned that the compass may show the first effects of a lack of horizontal directivity anywhere north of the 55th parallel. The effect is particularly vexing in rough weather, when the needle is constantly shifted from its point of equilibrium by the pitching and rolling of the vessel.

It may be noted in passing that what is true for the North Pole is also true for the South. By tradition, we generally mention the North Magnetic Pole as the source of the attraction which makes the magnetic compass work. But, as everyone will realise, the earth also possesses a South Magnetic Pole, and we could just as well say that it is this which attracts the compass needle. In reality, the North Magnetic Pole attracts the south pole of the compass needle, and the South Magnetic Pole attracts the north pole of the needle. The situation of the compass in the north or south magnetic hemisphere decides which Magnetic Pole has the predominating influence.

As far as horizontal directivity is concerned, the two attractions lie in the same line, and reinforce each other; but the same is not true of vertical directivity. In the northern magnetic hemisphere, the south pole of the needle points downwards, while the north pole of the needle points downward in the southern magnetic hemisphere.

From a practical point of view, the fact that the North Pole is predominant in one hemisphere and the South Pole in the other means that the navigator must turn over the vertical magnet which corrects the error due to heeling whenever he crosses the magnetic equator. In the northern hemisphere, to correct an error of this kind the origin of which is below the compass (as is generally the case), the south pole of the magnet (which is marked in red) must point upwards.

It should also be noted that the value of the vertical component of magnetic attraction is connected with the distance between the compass and the North Pole. This distance is expressed by the latitude; and that is why the correction for the error due to heel must be adjusted according to the latitude. The further north one goes, the more significant this error becomes; all the more so because the horizontal directivity weakens at the same time, so that the error ceases to be counterbalanced. The compass finally becomes completely useless, the slightest roll inducing a significant heeling error. It should be noted that heeling error is greatest when the boat's heading lies along a North–South axis; it decreases progressively as it departs from this axis, until the error is nil on a heading due East or West.

The gyroscopic compass, the functioning of which is based on the rotation of our planet around its axis, also gradually loses its directivity as one goes further north. It is therefore also unsuitable for arctic navigation.

Finally, the astro-compass provides the answer. This is an instrument based on visual observation, which can tell the navigator the direction in which he is sailing, if he observes any heavenly body whose declination and hour-angle are known to him. (He must also know the approximate latitude at which the observation is taken.)

Failing an astro-compass, an alidade will do very well instead. The main difference between the two is that the astro-compass does not require any calculations, whereas the use of the alidade does involve the calculation of azimuths, which means either consulting tables or using an electronic calculator.

The Sextant

Astronomical observation remains (with dead reckoning) the most reliable way of finding position out of sight of land. To the north of the arctic circle, however, the use of the traditional sextant is subject to certain restrictions, due among other things to the absence of a precise horizon over stretches of ice the surface of which has been made irregular by convergent pressure, to the effects of mirage and to the existence of false horizons, which are particularly common in the Arctic. The solution is to fit the sextant with an artificial horizon, which can generally be obtained as an accessory; alternatively a bubble sextant can be bought in the first place. Among the difficulties which a sextant with artificial horizon cannot remove, we must mention those due to frequent fogs and snowstorms. Refraction also poses problems, owing to the fact that most of the heavenly bodies are low in the sky; significant corrections for this factor are necessary, and are not always easy to evaluate. The use of a sextant with an artificial horizon is not easy on board a small vessel when it is under way. The lack of stability distorts the observation, which can really only be made in calm conditions. But if a ship is caught in the ice, or if her crew are faced with the problem of survival on land, a sextant with an artificial horizon may provide the most valuable service. It should also be noted that the effect of any error in the chronometer on one's calculated position becomes less and less as one approaches the North Pole. At the pole itself, time has in theory no effect on the calculated position at all.

For example, whereas at the equator an error in time of four seconds will cause an error of one mile in position, on the 70th parallel it will take an error of 18 seconds to produce the same result, and on the 80th parallel an error of 23 seconds would be needed for the same effect.

Cold and Ice

This may be the time to say a word about climatic conditions. The greatest obstacle to the North-West Passage arises from the dangers inherent in the ice movements. A word of explanation may be necessary here. At the meteorological station of Resolute Bay, which is a key point in the North-West Passage, only three months of the year have a mean temperature above freezing point—June with 32.5°F., July with 40°F. and August with 37°F.

This brief season of relative warmth obviously cannot bring about a complete melting of the ice (which can attain a thickness of more than five metres in the course of a single winter). It does however temporarily prevent ice floes which have been broken up by the action of tides, waves, winds or currents from freezing together again into a solid mass.

The waters of the Passage, extending over a distance of about 5000 miles, carry a mass of floating ice the mobility of which is governed by the various thrusts of currents and wind and by the geographical characteristics of the route. Without going into details which I shall be able to clear up in the course of my narrative, I think I can say that the key to success is largely to be found in the ability to form a general picture of the effects of the different factors which govern the movements of the ice at a given time. This ability makes it possible to make short-term predictions as necessary. The thing to avoid at all costs is getting caught in the ice. This involves many dangers. The first is that the boat may be crushed by the pressure of the ice if the pack drifts up against an obstacle. There is also the risk of being carried further to the north, where there is no seasonal thaw, and you may be imprisoned in the ice for an indefinite period . . . which could run into years. Finally, there is the danger that the boat will drift up against a submerged obstacle. This implies that the place chosen to spend the winter must have certain well defined characteristics. Since we know that drifting is dangerous, the first point is to establish the boat in a position where it can remain stationary. A landlocked bay is the best answer. For the safety of the boat, it is necessary that the bay should be protected by a wide, shallow bar. The bay must not freeze down to the bottom, for otherwise the thaw would take much longer, and part of the following season would be wasted by the consequent delay in departure. It does not matter if the water over the bar freezes to the bottom; the ice will be exposed to the effects of the waters inside and outside the bay, and we may assume that it will be broken up at the time of the general thaw in any case.

The necessity of finding a place protected by a shallow bar arises from the fact that about seven-tenths of the volume of floating ice remains below the surface. A shallow bar will therefore exclude all the larger masses of ice. The same consideration underlies the whole strategy of safe navigation in icy waters. It is often necessary to choose a course through shallow waters in order to find a way through the ice fields. As far as wintering is concerned, we may observe that the real danger to which the boat is exposed does not come from the freezing of the stretch of water in which it floats, but from the possible invasion of that stretch of water by large masses of ice, which would tower over the hull and crush it like a nut in a gigantic vice.

Information regarding the depth of the water is so vital that a good sounder is essential. *Williwaw* is equipped with an S.A.I.T. sounder, which indicates depths up to 400 metres below the keel. This is a very important safety factor.

(My equipment included some long-handled mallets to knock the ice off the rigging and avoid the risk of capsize through excess weight aloft, but icing was not a problem I encountered in the pack-ice: the danger comes from spray freezing in the rigging, which occurs chiefly in rough open waters.)

Whatever precautions you take, an accident is always possible, and it may, alas, become necessary to abandon ship. In that case, I have to think about survival on land.

I therefore considered it essential to include in my stores everything which is necessary for survival on shore, starting with some form of shelter. I am capable of building an igloo, and I might have decided that that was good enough; but not every type of snow is suitable for this kind of building, which also demands a considerable expenditure of physical energy; and so it would have been useful to take a double-walled nylon tent, treated against condensation, of the type used on mountain expeditions, and I had hoped to do this. But the cost of fitting out *Williwaw* obliged me to revise my budget, and in the end I had to do without this extremely useful piece of equipment.

One also has to eat—and eat well, for expenditure of calories is very high. For obvious reasons, the food must be easy to carry. The British Antarctic Survey expeditions have developed a light-weight pack of dehydrated rations put up in small boxes, which contain all that a man needs for twenty days at an energy consumption rate of 4800 calories per day. I had planned to take from ten to twenty boxes, according to the space I had available; this would have given me enough food to ensure survival outside the boat for more than 200 days. I have not however been able to do so, for the same reason which prevented me from buying the tent I wanted.

It is true that I have studied the arts of seal-hunting and of catching fish. I have all the necessary equipment on board; but I have a profound respect for animal life, and I shall only use it in the event of absolute necessity.

To enable me to transport indispensable stores, I have a collapsible sledge. I have, of course, no dogs on board. I say 'of course', because it would be difficult to find room for their food, and it must be admitted that life on a small boat would not suit them very well. This is a pity, for dogs can be very useful. A dog can keep you warm—you can snuggle him in your sleeping-bag if you are cold. He can also satisfy your hunger! But I dislike the idea so much that I prefer not to take the risk.

To avoid a tedious catalogue, I have not mentioned everything which is necessary for survival. One obviously has to have a primus stove, fuel, suitable clothing, etc. All the experts emphasise the close connection between exposure to the wind and loss of bodily heat. Adequate protection against the wind is therefore essential. Cheeks and nose are very vulnerable, and one is advised to pass one's hand across one's face at regular intervals to detect any possible onset of frostbite. If any part of the face freezes hard, you must defrost it immediately by covering it with the bare hand and sheltering it from the wind. Avoid the stupid mistake of rubbing a frostbite with snow; sound tissue will be favourably stimulated by rubbing with snow, but frostbitten tissue is beyond such stimulation and requires above all an application of warmth to surrounding areas.

Never lose sight of the fact that hands and feet have absolute priority in the matter of protection. For special clothing to be worn at sea, I put my faith in 'Equinoxe', whose products I know well, having used them on my voyage around the world.

The Boat and her Equipment

Williwaw has been carefully modified for arctic navigation. The stem has been reinforced and lengthened so that it projects in front of the bobstay, protecting it. The angle of this new stem has been designed so that the potential energy developed by running into floating ice will be dissipated by a thrust tending to lift the weight of the boat.

Heat insulation has been very thoroughly carried out with glass wool, and there is now no direct contact between the outer shell of the boat and the air inside her.

An adequate temperature is assured by several different kinds of heater, including a fuel-oil stove of the type used on board Norwegian trawlers, and a warm-air heater whose special task is to heat the engine compartment, which contains not only the main engine but a 24-volt generator to charge the batteries while we are laid up for the winter, and a 220-volt generator to supply the tools of the little workshop which I have on board—compressor, grinder, drill and so on. I also have a windmill generator which can develop 300 watts.

Diesel-oil, which solidifies at low temperatures, has been replaced by kerosene as a fuel for both motors and heating. I have already had occasion to mention the radar and the radio equipment. I shall certainly have more to say about them later, for both of them are regularly in service.

I have now begun to put into sober operation a project which previously looked like a reckless gamble. I have put a lot of effort into the considerable amount of research involved, and I truly believe that I have made the very best preparations of which I am capable.

None the less, as I realise very well, the imponderable and the unknown still lie in wait; a summer without any thaw, a sudden, incapacitating illness, a hazard which is not shown on the chart . . . Who knows what may happen? So ought I to resign myself to giving up my project? I do not think so. To reject the imponderable is to reject life itself.

8

Davis Strait:
a First Encounter with the Ice

Coming on deck at about 2 in the morning after passing the night
hove-to, I can clearly see the jagged skyline of Greenland against
the light to the east. The sun is still hidden behind the mountains
which tower above the region of Frederikshaab, which is swathed
in a light mist. The sky, reddening, outlines the violet hills with
flame. Though the troughs of the waves are still black, the sea
reddens to the rhythm of a gentle swell whose crests bring with
them the flamboyant reality of the dawn.

Little by little, the sun climbs the peaks; the sky grows lighter
and so does the earth. The contrast between the two weakens, and
Greenland gently disappears again. It has only been visible for a
few minutes, and I have not even had the time to feel cold.

The peace of the morning takes possession of me, and I stay on
deck a little longer, feeling, as so often before, that Nature is very
near to me, and that I am part of her. The same question always
comes to me spontaneously on these occasions; I regard it as a
matter of course, and do not pay too much attention to it. Sometimes, however, I try to find a rational answer, and address the
question firmly to my intelligence, which dodges it or rejects it,
and never answers it at all. I know very well that the chemists are
trying to explain the origin of life, and that one day they may have
the power to create it. But that makes no difference—they won't
be able to tell me where that power comes from!

My landfall is right on target; but isn't that due to the perfectly
coordinated movements of the stars? I have doubtless done my bit
as well, I do not deny it; but isn't man a part of creation just as
much as the stars? And who or what guided the pigeon towards the
land? Who or what!—always the same question. Shall I discover
the answer some day?

I go below and cook myself a good meal. Well wrapped up, for it
is very cold, I proceed on my way as soon as I have finished eating.

At 0930 I suddenly notice an iceberg on the port bow. This is a big moment: my first iceberg, my first real encounter with the ice. The radar tells me that it is nine miles off. The echo is good, and improves as time goes by. At six miles it is excellent. I had not been able to get any definite information in advance about the quality of radar signals as reflected by icebergs, but now I know. Radar will warn me adequately when icebergs are there. I take some photographs as I sail past. A pleasant souvenir of a first meeting!

Towards midday the sky becomes overcast, and the sun is not visible at noon. Several icebergs are now in sight. I cross the path of a fishing vessel bound for the coast. No doubt she is going to Frederikshaab. So I have won my bet with Albert. Today is June 12, and he had to be back in Belgium by the seventeenth; so I could have dropped him off at Frederikshaab in plenty of time. What a pity that Albert did not have more faith in his lucky star—or in the sterling qualities of *Williwaw*! I should have liked to have kept him with me.

I sight several more icebergs during the afternoon. I am sorry to note that although the icebergs themselves send back a good echo, the growlers which they spawn all around them do not show up on the radar screen. As these 'small' pieces of ice which split off from the icebergs can easily weigh a few dozen tons, so that a collision could do a lot of damage, I have to remain on watch all the time. Several times I have to swerve violently at the last moment, and so I discover that growlers are not easy to pick out in the distance. I am going to have to keep on my toes! (I discover later on that it depends on the state of the sea whether growlers can be detected or not. With a calm sea they show up; with a rough sea, their echo is lost in the sea clutter.)

At about 1800 I heave-to again. The wind has fallen, and I reckon that a good night's sleep will do me no harm. After a good supper and a look round the horizon with the radar, I go to sleep. The time is 1930, and the nearest iceberg is five miles away.

I don't know what wakes me up—possibly the noise of water running past the hull. I leap out on to the deck, and am amazed to see that the boat is under way. How can this have happened? I am quite certain that I locked the helm right over to the starboard side. *Williwaw* is equipped with a hydraulic rudder control, and a series of valves normally fixes the rudder-blade in the required position. Some defect must have made it possible for the rudder to swing back in line with the axis of the boat, and for the boat to get under way. I at once check the working of the rudder control, and soon realise that one of the piston washers must be leaking. This is serious, but not disastrous. The control mechanism is still working. The only thing is that I cannot now heave to except by using the emergency helm, which I shall have to lash to one side.

Busy with checking the control mechanism, I have forgotten to note the course on which the boat was sailing when I woke up. This is a serious mistake; how can I now estimate my present position?

The sun now sinks below the horizon only for a few hours every night. On June 14, the sun rose at 0211 and set at 2149. The night is not really dark, and the twilights of evening and morning run into each other. It is broad daylight when we proceed on our route. The north wind brings with it a fine rain mixed with melting snow. It is unpleasant weather, grey, damp and cold. Sea and sky shade into each other and the mist hides the horizon as well as the land. My hands are cold: warm, waterproof gloves are as rare as white whales. The best policy is to put on woollen gloves and to wear rubber mittens over them. I tack towards the coast keeping an eye on my radar and echo-sounder. This increases my bewilderment. The information provided by the sounder does not correspond at all to the information on the chart at my estimated position. Try as I may, I cannot find out where I am. *Williwaw* must have covered quite a distance while I was asleep, but in which direction? In order to keep out of trouble while I am trying to work things out, I turn out to sea again and sail six miles on a bearing of $325°$, and then twelve miles on a bearing of $60°$. After this I learn from the radar that the coast is nine miles away. Still unable to find my position, I turn out to sea once more. My uncertainty continues until the sun comes out for a short time and I manage to take a sight. The position line plotted on the chart places me much further north than expected. I must have drifted up-wind—this means that the current is very strong.

I knew, of course, that a northerly set fringes the western coast of Greenland. But it had not seemed to me to be very strong during the previous few days, and I had not expected this sudden increase in speed. I check the facts in the *Sailing Directions*, and find that at certain times (not otherwise specified), the current may exceed 3 knots.

This is a relatively warm current, and causes the sea to thaw along the coast of Greenland earlier than along the Canadian coast. Hence my choice of route.

My noon position today, June 14, was 62° 43' N., 51° 05' W.

The compass still seems to me to have an adequate amount of directivity, and I can navigate with the automatic pilot. During the afternoon, I am busy in the engine compartment, and change a leaky washer on the main engine's heat exchanger. The leak only showed up when we started up the engine from cold—during the brief period when the thermostat stops the water circulating, and the pressure in the heat exchanger is consequently at the highest level. I therefore had a devil of a time pin-pointing the trouble. It should also be mentioned that I could only spend a few minutes at a time below because of the number of icebergs in the area.

Towards the end of the day, I use the radar to find a gap among the icebergs where I can spend the night in relative safety, and as the wind has dropped I lower the sails and let the boat drift. Shortly afterwards I am sleeping like a baby. The alarm clock wakes me up, as planned, two hours later. I check my position in relation to the icebergs, and am surprised to see that the boat is drifting appreciably faster than they are. Before I went to sleep, I had carefully made a plan of the various echoes which appeared on the radar screen, and now I notice that the picture has completely changed. The iceberg which was four miles ahead is now only two miles away, and another, which was one mile away from the first, has now put an interval of three miles between them. What is happening? Not only is *Williwaw* moving at a different speed from the icebergs, but they are moving at different speeds from each other!

The echo-sounder indicates 44 fathoms, equivalent to about 80 metres. A glance at the chart shows me that I am on the edge of the Danas Bank. Most of the icebergs on the starboard side must be drawing enough water to bring them quite close to the sea floor, in these circumstances. Some of them ought to be running aground now, to judge by their size. A regularly shaped block of ice which rises 15 metres above the surface will have a draught of about 60 metres. The current is generally stronger at the surface than near the bottom, where its speed is reduced by friction; icebergs drifting in shallow water therefore move more slowly than those in deep water. On the port side, the water gets rapidly deeper, and the icebergs on that side naturally drift at a higher speed.

That explains why each iceberg has its own personal speed of drift. Little by little I am learning what I need to know!

Experience is something which in fact has to be actively pursued. It is not a gift which comes with age, but a prize to be won by method. We achieve it by keeping our eyes open and analysing what we see. A sailor who does not regularly check his course, for example, loses the chance of learning something valuable every time he makes this omission.

Our observed position at noon on June 14 is 63° 14' N., 51° 48' W. We are over the Fiskenaes Bank, in 50 fathoms. The temperature is 50°F. Last night it went down to 39°F. There is a light wind from the north. Barometer at 1015 millibars and falling. Sea calm. Several big icebergs aground on the edge of the Bank. The coast is not in sight.

I keep sailing all through the night to take advantage of a light wind from the south-east. In the morning the wind strengthens and stays at force 5. The sky is overcast and it is raining, but we have made good progress. The sun is not visible at noon on June 15. With a constantly overcast sky, dead reckoning comes into its own, though I use the echo-sounder as a check—the geography of the sea bottom in these parts has a definite and varied pattern, which often makes it possible for me to fix my position exactly. Every time we cross a submarine contour of 50 or 100 fathoms the fact is carefully noted on the chart. Mounted on the rail aft, my reliable Excelsior log records the distance covered. Every week I take its rotator out of the water and examine it. If necessary, I shorten the line, which can easily become worn where it joins both the sinker and the rotator.

We passed Godhaab during the night, but visibility is poor and I am much too far out to be able to see the coast. I watch the radar all through the following night, with only short snatches of sleep. (I make every effort to conform to a regular daily pattern of life; but if I run into an iceberg my journey will come to an abrupt end, and prudence is necessary.)

It is snowing on the morning of the 16th, and I cross the Arctic Circle in a squall. I open a half-bottle of champagne, a present from the 'Frères de la Côte' at Brussels. There is no need for an ice-bucket; it is perfectly chilled already.

No noon sight on the 16th. We are sailing over the extensive Hellefiske Bank, which is fortunately quite shallow, and so does not allow the passage of icebergs. After a fine night, the sky is over-cast again on the morning of the 17th. The temperature is down to 30°F.

I make my plans to reach land, as the latitude of Egedesminde is now quite close. I make use of the 100-fathom contour on the north side of the Hellefiske Bank as the starting point for my coastal route. I no longer have complete confidence in the compass, and I want to reinsure myself against error in every way before I sight land. Luckily the sun comes through the layer of stratus at the right moment, and I can check my route with the sextant. The land, at first enveloped in a thick curtain of mist, progressively becomes more visible, and I can identify the radar echoes with the real features they represent. There is Vester Island, my first land-mark on the way in to Egedesminde. It is a magnificent scene; the ocean is again that deep blue colour which we love to see. The distant land is tinted with mauve. One or two motionless icebergs complete the range of cool tones, while Vester Island, with its beaches of golden sand, adds warmth to the picture.

I find the line of the channel which leads to Egedesminde with-out difficulty. The harbour and the village remain out of sight behind an island for a long time. It is only after rounding the island that, with my back to the sun, I can see the brightly coloured wooden houses.

Boats put off from the shore. A group of youngsters invades the deck. An Eskimo vehemently reproaches me for not having hoisted the Danish flag; the harbour-master examines my papers. They all talk at once. After a moment's hesitation I anchor. I have spent 28 days at sea, and now I am in port again.

9

At Egedesminde

The first few days at Egedesminde are not exactly restful. The reason for this is simple enough. My arrival has coincided with the beginning of the weekend, when, traditionally, all the inhabitants are on their toes—all those who are sober enough to stand, at least . . . People drink a lot, dance a lot, and visit each other's homes. No-one bothers about time at the weekend, and I have an uninterrupted stream of visitors. All day and all night!

I try to be conciliatory. I give civil answers to questions (as far as I can understand them, not knowing Danish). I show people over the boat and get rid of them politely as soon as I can. There is no malice about the Eskimos, but they are somewhat offhand! They bring their beer with them, and clearly intend to stay until their thirst is finally quenched.

When Sunday night comes, I think I have finished with the visits, so I am not particularly pleased to be woken up the following morning by someone knocking on the hull.

'Ah, no! Not again!'

With a determined gesture, I open the hatch and find myself face to face with a middle-aged native carrying a briefcase, who announces that he is a journalist. He points at a little boy, scarcely ten years old, and introduces him with the words 'my photographer'.

Prompted by his elder, the lad nods his head: yes, he's the photographer all right! He has a camera slung round his neck, which bumps against his shins. 'What is all this?', I wonder.

My unknown visitor speaks English with a sort of glib facility. Disarmed by the funny side of the situation, I let them in. The journalist has mentioned his name but I have not taken it in. As soon as he sits down he tells me, with a smile, that he has not come unprepared. He opens his briefcase and takes out, not a notebook, but a bottle!

'Ah, no! What a beginning!' But he turns out to be a pleasant and quite well educated man, and we are soon deep in conversation. Kununguak Fleischer (I have persuaded him to write his name down on a piece of paper) is a teacher and also runs a small school newspaper, on behalf of which he has come to interview me. The school has a small photographic laboratory, where he teaches his pupils to develop black and white pictures—hence the 'photographer' who has come with him.

During our conversation, I say that I imagine that drink must be one of his most serious educational problems, for it is a pity to see the abuse of alcohol prevailing so widely. But Kununguak Fleischer seems to hold moderate views; he does not dramatise the situation, and is full of concern for his brother Eskimos.

Kununguak is the bearer of an invitation to dinner from his wife, and before he leaves me he insists on my accepting. He will come and fetch me this evening, and we can go on together to the hotel where we shall eat. I begin by telling him that I am very tired, but he is so insistent that I end up by accepting.

At the time agreed, Kununguak picks me up; first of all we go to his house, for a little aperitif, as he puts it. Pierke, his wife, who is extremely pretty, is waiting for us. By way of welcome, she offers me a piece of whale-blubber, or *matak*, with the inevitable Carlsberg. I wish I could escape, not because of Pierke, but because of the prospect of having to swallow raw whale-blubber. I try it in the end, out of politeness and also out of curiosity, but I do not take a second mouthful, and I am relieved when Kununguak says it is time to go.

The restaurant comprises several large rooms and a dance floor. Kununguak has invited some other friends of his, and there are about ten of us at table. The basis of the dinner is reindeer meat; it is washed down with a great deal to drink, and I conclude that education against alcoholism is not Kununguak's top priority. None of the guests seems to have much of a head for drink, and I have some difficulty in keeping my own rate of consumption down to a reasonable level. Towards the end of the meal, the music begins and several women join our table—God knows where they come from! All of them want to dance with me, but the average age of these ladies is really discouraging. The youngest is at least fifteen years older than myself. As far as politeness permits, I try to decline their invitations. When they insist, I tell Kununguak, who I notice is no longer in a fit state to take me back to the boat, that I want to go to bed. (My own dinghy is still on *Williwaw*'s deck.) He asks one of his friends, Partapik, to take me back. As we leave the table, four terrible female figures follow close on our heels! On the way to the harbour, the boldest of the four grabs me by the arm, and is at once overwhelmed with curses by the other three. The scene is difficult to describe—you need to see the characters! I burst out laughing, which adds to the general confusion. I somehow manage to free my arm, urge Partapik forwards, and walk faster. Behind us the women are still quarrelling, and are ready to come to blows. What a business! When we reach the harbour, I slow up to let my guide let slip the dinghy, take a run and jump aboard.

My pursuers, who are evidently not in very good training, have been left behind, and we leave the shore without any further difficulty. Partapik does not utter a word. Anxious to avoid offending both parties, he does not utter a word right up to the end of the adventure. Back on the quay, four little old women out of a horror film are pulling one another's hair. The unexpected plays a large part in my dealings with the Eskimos!

Returning to more serious matters, I am relieved to learn the following morning that the cassettes have arrived. This is good news, and removes a serious source of worry. It also reminds me that so far I have had practically no time to use my camera. How am I going to be able to complete my film? It is not likely that the conditions of navigation are going to become easier—quite the contrary in fact. It is not simply a matter of shooting the film; I have not written a single newspaper article since I left.

This naturally leads me to size up my ability to make a good job of this project. The navigation has turned out to be very taxing; it has nothing in common with sailing in the trade-wind belt. The North Atlantic gave me a hard time, and icebergs present undoubted problems to the single-handed navigator, keeping him on watch all night—though icebergs floating in the open sea are incomparably less dangerous than pack-ice.

So I am not trying to dodge the problem. My resistance has its limits, and the fatigue resulting from a long period of overstrain cannot be cured by a short spell in port. The experience gained in the first part of the voyage has clearly shown me that I am going to find it difficult, during the very short open season, to keep two things going at once: on the one hand, the navigation of the boat, and on the other the activity which is intended to provide for the financing of the expedition, and so to make it possible for it to go on. The fact must be faced: leaving the beaten track can cost you a lot of money.

If a man wanted to fit out an expedition in the sixteenth century, he applied to Charles V or Queen Elizabeth. But nowadays a journey of this sort has to finance itself. This fact is not unwelcome to me; it agrees very well with my desire for self-sufficiency. But shooting a film, or writing a book or a series of articles requires a great deal of care and a great deal of time. Yet life on a sailing vessel is very active: it is not just a matter of covering a certain distance, but also of making good wear and tear, painting what rusts, and cleaning what gets dirty. All in all, I realise that it would be easier for two people than it is for me on my own.

During my preliminary studies, before I set out, I paid a visit one evening to a Belgian family who are famous for their experience in the field of arctic exploration. Two sons of the family were there, and at the end of the evening both of them expressed an interest in my project and offered to come with me—without really having made up their minds to it, as I thought at the time.

I did not expect this conversation to have any result. I was therefore surprised when Jean-Louis, who had come to Nieuport to see me off, told me that he would really like to come with me. Since I was on the point of putting to sea, it was obviously not possible for me to accept his offer, and we left it at that. I must also mention that, once I had announced my project, a number of people offered to come with me. But however much warmth and fellow-feeling might be expressed in these offers, I never took them up, for I know how difficult it is to set up a tightly-knit team in the enforced intimacy of a small boat.

However, in present circumstances, I decide to let Jean-Louis know that I am ready to offer him a place on board. He is the grandson of Adrien de Gerlache, who commanded the Belgian polar expedition of 1897–99 during which the three-master *Belgica* became the first ship to winter in the Antarctic; he is also the son of Gaston de Gerlache, who was the leader of the Antarctic expedition of 1957–59; so he should be sufficiently motivated to share the hardships and dangers of our common venture. I should be very pleased to be able to offer a member of his family a fresh opportunity of getting to grips with the world of snow and ice on which they have already spent so much effort. The addition of Jean-Louis to the party would also fit in well with my wish to give my project a Belgian connection.

For devious administrative reasons, I am of Dutch nationality; but I was born and I have spent my whole life in Belgium. Belgium is the land where my children, my family and my friends all live, and the land where I keep my dreams. The Dutch flag may wave proudly over my ketch, but I think it only right that my heart should fly the colours of Belgium.

Several days have gone by since I landed at Egedesminde. I have had the opportunity to visit the village a couple of times and to see what goes on there. The Greenland Eskimo is a traditionalist where food is concerned. All day long, small fishing vessels come into port carrying fish, whale-meat, seal-meat or sea birds, according to what they have caught. All this is sold at the quay-side. The Danes follow a more European diet, but some of them like whale-meat, which is not unlike beef. Danes are regularly to be seen among the other customers on the quay. I notice that they always seem to pay higher prices than the Eskimo, though the Eskimo gets away with the best pieces.

This is a practical expression in everyday relationships of the hostility of the Greenlanders towards the Danes, and, by extension towards all foreigners of a different race from their own. This hostility, reinforced by alcoholism, regularly leads to brawls, and the average Dane, not wishing to make things worse, finds it best to stay at home in the evening, especially at the weekend, when the beer is flowing freely.

It must be realised that firearms for hunting purposes are on open sale, and that a child of twelve or over can buy any sort of rifle.It is easy to understand that 'accidents' happen and that it is best to be careful. The hostility is particularly bitter among the young Eskimos, who are the most violent.

It must also be noted that life is cheap in the eyes of the Eskimo, and that his view is supported by the penal code in force in Greenland. Generally speaking the maximum penalty for murder is not more than five years of imprisonment, in a modern jail with television, cinema, games and paid work outside the walls. To our way of thinking—since compassion is part of our civilization—the

Eskimo is equally cruel towards animals, which he kills thought-lessly, and often needlessly.

It is common practice in Greenland to take one's sledge dogs at the time of the spring thaw, and to leave them without food on one of the rocky desert islands which fringe the coast until the end of the summer, in order to let natural selection operate to the full. Dogs are also killed for their fur, which is used to make warm foot-coverings to be worn underneath sealskin boots. The dog is gene-rally hanged, because this makes the fur stand up better.

Luckily very little is now made by hand in Greenland apart from boots and gloves. Otherwise the Eskimo dresses in synthetic fibres, just like the European. The shops are full of every kind of article, and well known brands of beauty products are on sale every-where. This may surprise the reader, but I must add that Eskimo women are often very pretty—when they are young!

I am conscious of the fact that I have not given a very engaging picture of the inhabitants of Egedesminde. But I have restricted myself to facts which are easy to check, and have refrained from passing any judgments.

I have mentioned conditions in the prison at Egedesminde, which is one of the most modern in Greenland, because I saw them for myself when I visited the place. The death-agony of the dogs is such a noisy business that no-one who spends any time near the village could fail to be aware of it.

If I generally avoid mingling my personal views with facts such as those I have just described, this is in the first place because, as a matter of principle, I do not regard myself as called on to judge other men, and in the second place because I have no pretensions to being a moralist or a qualified anthropologist.

Having said all that, I will not conceal the fact that I am always revolted to see the constant, implacable, idiotic and cruel aggres-sion of which animals are the victims—especially animals which have an economic value. In my view, to destroy life is immoral and contrary to the teachings of Nature, unless the destruction of one life is redeemed by the safeguarding of another.

10

The J. E. Bernier II *and the Arrival*
of Jean-Louis

A day or two ago, I met the crew of the *J. E. Bernier II*, a sloop which set out from Montreal last year with the same object as myself—to complete the North-West Passage. The first season does not seem to have turned out very well for them, for they were compelled to lay up their vessel for the winter at Holsteinborg, about one hundred miles to the south of Egedesminde. The crew went back to Montreal for the winter, leaving the *Bernier* in Greenland.

I had heard about this 'rival' expedition shortly before setting out, and I was very interested to meet Réal Bouvier and his crew. They must have been equally interested in my project; having left their vessel in Greenland and gone back to Montreal for the winter, they had read in the press about my departure. Each of us was obviously curious about the abilities and the equipment of the other. But we avoided all outward signs of the competitive spirit. Our meetings, both on board *Williwaw* and on the *Bernier* were extremely cordial.

The crew consisted of four men and one woman. Under the benevolent eye of her captain, the enchanting Marie-Eve gave me their spare copy of the Canadian *Sailing Directions* and a maple-leaf courtesy ensign—which was something I had not brought with me.

I felt very strongly that this present brought with it a shining example of fair play, and I resolved to do as much for them at the first opportunity.

These Canadians were very charming—and also very confident. As regards confidence, I was a little surprised by the lighthearted way in which they spoke about the difficulties of the voyage. To hear them talk, Bering Strait might already be in sight!

The boat itself reflects this optimism to some extent. There is no interior insulation against the cold, and large areas of bare steel can be seen when you go below. The captain can't have given any serious thought to spending the winter on board. At low temperatures, condensation must be a big problem. Altogether, I prefer my *Williwaw*. The *Bernier* only stayed one day in harbour. They have gone off to film the glaciers near Jacobshavn. I am waiting for Jean-Louis to arrive. I had a radio call this morning to say that he had spent the evening with my friend Guy. Jean-Louis will bring a tent and some extra winter clothing. My original invitation referred only to the crossing of Baffin Bay; but Guy quite rightly says that, since Jean-Louis will have to give up his job, I ought to take him on for the whole season. The fact is that, not knowing Jean-Louis at all well, I did not want to commit myself too far in advance. Provided that there is no serious incompatibility between us, he can of course stay on board as long as he likes. I stipulate, in any case, that each of us must be free to cancel the arrangement at any time—trusting, of course, that we are both mature enough not to take such a decision lightly.

As I can see nothing in my proposals which is likely to raise any problem, I look forward to Jean-Louis's arrival in the near future. I have complete confidence in Guy, who has plenty of experience, and knows all about life on board and the mental attitude required. I accept in advance any detailed arrangements which Guy may make.

My time in port is beginning to drag a little, and I have nothing to gain from a further stay. I have filled up with fuel and water. All the equipment is in perfect condition. Kununguak regularly comes to see me, and always asks me to have a drink with him; but for some time now I have been refusing his invitations as politely as possible. For Kununguak, the proceedings invariably end in almost complete unconsciousness, and it is very difficult to bring the party to an end.

Some young fellows have come and demanded drugs. They were angry when I told them that I hadn't got any. One of them threw a handful of bank notes on the cabin table and said 'There!... Do you think that we can't pay you?' I conclude that other boats do bring drugs in here. What a wretched business! I cannot wait to get out into the pure atmosphere of the open sea. Jean-Louis finally arrives on July 8, after a delay caused by the persistent mist which has covered Egedesminde for several days. According to the captain of the *Bamsa Dan*, a cargo-ship which supplies this region, the state of the ice should permit us to reach Upernavik, 400 miles further north. So we can make some useful progress, and I am impatient to get into action again after my long spell in harbour.

To give my companion a little time to acclimatise himself, we spend Saturday July 9 adjusting the compass. There are several good transits at Egedesminde and also an expanse of water which is sheltered enough for the work to be done in favourable conditions. The lack of directivity slows up the movements of the needle, and it takes an age to get it stabilised. But with patience one can succeed, and I am not dissatisfied with the result.

Everything is new for Jean-Louis. He has never sailed on a yacht before. We put to sea on the morning of July 10, in fair weather, with a clear sky and good visibility. The barometer is steady at 1017 millibars, and the temperature about midday is 46°F. A light head-wind compels us to tack; a few hours later the breeze drops completely, and I have no hesitation in starting the engine. We must press on.

It should be mentioned that these periods of calm are quite common on the west coast of Greenland, and a good auxiliary engine is indispensable if you want to cover a given distance in a certain length of time. But refuelling can be a problem, and it is best to use sail whenever possible.

On the morning of the 11th, I am annoyed to discover that one of the engine securing bolts has sheared right across—a steel bolt 14 mm in diameter! I decide to run into Mellemfjord, a small inlet on the western coast of Disco Island, and we drop anchor there in the course of the afternoon. But alas, the defect cannot be rectified without taking out the engine, which is a task I cannot undertake at the moment. As soon as possible, probably at Upernavik, we shall have to weld the securing bracket directly on to the framework. That is all we can hope to do in the time available. We remain at anchor for the night, and go on the following morning.

As we come out of the fjord, we are greeted by a force 4 wind from the north-west, and the barometer shows 1015 millibars, falling rapidly. The temperature is 43°F. After we have sailed close-hauled for several miles, the wind veers to the east, and we greet the change with three cheers. The new wind is light at first, but increases rapidly. I am probably underestimating the shelter afforded by the coast, for as soon as we arrive opposite the opening of the Vaigat (the channel which separates Disco Island from Nugssuaq Peninsula), *Williwaw*—still under full sail—is knocked down by a squall.

We quickly hand the staysail, and then the mizzen. The strength of the wind makes it difficult to keep the boat under control. The waters of the Vaigat contain a large number of icebergs coming down from the glaciers of Jacobshavn, and *Williwaw* has to thread her way between them. There is very little open water, and no time to waste. I turn down-wind so that I can lower the jib. The squalls are violent and prolonged. We have put on our oilskins, and are soon soaked in sweat. At first I think this is solely due to our violent exertions, but later, when things slacken off, I realise that the temperature has become astonishingly warm—over 68°F.

With only mainsail and storm-jib, we are still carrying too much sail. The anemometer indicates force 9 just before a squall of force 10, 11 or more hits us. I try to run before the wind, but an enormous iceberg is in the way, and we are sailing near the wind as I signal to Jean-Louis to lower the mainsail. But the halyard jams and the sail stays up. The canvas beats furiously against the shrouds. The battens shatter and pierce the canvas, and the leech literally disintegrates. What a disaster! My fine main-sail, which has taken me round the world, destroyed in a few seconds—and it's all my fault! Jean-Louis does his best to sort out the tangle of ropes, and I leave the helm and help him to haul the sail. With only the storm-jib up, the boat finally becomes more manageable. We rapidly lash the sails on deck and then hoist the trysail.

When the wind drops, the temperature falls as well. We have seen what happens when a mass of warm air from the tropics passes inside the Arctic Circle. Jean-Louis—have I mentioned that he had no previous experience of sailing?—took this first, terrifying adventure very stoically.

The cold front which has overtaken us now brings rain, melting snow, fog and low temperature. The wind on the other hand is much lighter. Such are the weather conditions when we reach the latitude of the Svartenhuk Peninsula.

A gloomy landscape appears dimly in the distance. The great icebergs, looming larger than life in the drizzle, are haloed with a whitish blink, and Svartenhuk Peninsula can just be made out in a large patch of shadow. As so often, there is no dividing line between sky and sea in the pallid light of morning. Every time I go below to consult the chart, the water accumulated in the canvas trickles off the mizzen boom in a thin steady stream which finds its way, on the port tack, inside the cabin. I don't care for it to rain on board *Williwaw*!

Towards the end of the morning, the wind gets progressively lighter, and the lack of sail makes itself felt. I hate to see my boat dawdle; I hate not to get all the mileage possible out of the wind. I love it when the boat cuts her way through the water, wings outstretched, with a vibration I can feel in my bones; I love the sound of the water running along the side, and the sight of our bow-wave which marks out our mighty wake far astern.

This reinforces my longing to find an anchorage where we can bend on the spare mainsail. Midlorfik Fjord, a small inlet to the north of the peninsula, well protected from the weather by Skalø Island, should offer us an excellent place in which to shelter. It seems to be easy to find, easy to enter, and extremely safe. I have often noticed how few sailors really take advantage of all that charts have to offer—how few can quickly find where to land on an unknown coast. Very often a careful study of the chart would give them information which can be interpreted without the help of any instrument. To find the entrance to Midlorfik Fjord, for example, the chart shows that all you have to do is to sail towards the coast along the transit connecting the main headlands on the south-east coast of Skalø Island. What could be simpler?

In most cases, the chart will reveal an easily recognized mark, a transit which can be followed, or a useful line of soundings. All you have to do is to examine the chart carefully. And with a little practice one soon learns to improve one's visualisation of the information it contains—in other words to imagine the appearance of a coast by reading its main features, and to work out a simple and easy plan for finding one's destination from the topography shown.

A few stranded growlers indicate the presence of a shallow bar at the entry to Midlorfik Fjord. Jean-Louis watches the echo-sounder, while I steer for a small cove where we shall be protected from drifting ice. The bottom shelves gradually, without the irregularities that indicate rocks or coral reefs.

'Seven fathoms!'

'Let's anchor!' Having anchored, we begin by awarding ourselves a few hours' rest—'well-earned rest', I add, with a touch of
smugness. Then we bend on the new sail, and finally lower the
dinghy for a short visit to the shore. It turns out to be a very short
one, for a cloud of mosquitoes attacks us immediately. Flies and
mosquitoes are a plague in the Arctic; they come after you in vast
swarms. After taking a few pictures, we have to retreat to the boat.
Knowing that mosquitoes do not cross wide expanses of water, I
have not anchored too close to the shore, and once on board we are
safe from their attention.

11

Upernavik and Kraulshavn

The next day, July 15, we set out again, with the new mainsail up. The weather has cleared. My sailor's instinct normally prompts me to follow a course well away from the coast, but today I take the inner passage, for the chart does not give full information about soundings in the area around Upernavik. Soundings are marked only along the route among the coastal islands, and this is the one we follow.

It is a wonderful scenic route; and the multitude of islands and the narrowness of the channels remind me of Patagonia. But the landscape itself is quite different, consisting entirely of earth, water and ice, without any vegetation. There is nothing corresponding to the cordillera of the Andes which dominates the jagged landscape down there in the far south. But the glaciers are more numerous here, and, if the landscape is less hair-raising, the temperature makes us shiver. We are lucky enough only to meet with one or two patches of open pack-ice near Store Fladø Island, and we reach Upernavik on the same day (Friday July 15). The sun, which at this time of year moves a little further away to the south every day, is still shining despite the lateness of the hour. A little later, at midnight (local time), we can see the sun at a height of $4° 38'$ above the horizon at this latitude, which is $72° 47'$ N. (At the summer solstice, on June 21, it reached its maximum midnight elevation for this year, at $6° 13'$.)

The fact that the sun never sets makes it theoretically possible for the navigator to take two meridian altitudes every twenty-four hours: one at midday, when the sun is south at its highest point, and one at midnight when it is north at its lowest. At the North Pole, the sun moves in a more horizontal fashion, and its elevation coincides with its declination. The midnight altitude is therefore practically the same as that at midday. Today the declination being $21° 25'$ N. at 0000 hours, that is also the altitude of the sun at the North Pole.

Upernavik is an Eskimo village of about 500 souls, built on a hill overhanging a small bay which serves as a harbour. The brightly coloured wooden houses are arranged in terraces up the slope to the top, from which an unmetalled track leads down to a small landing quay. The port installations consist of the quay, some buoys and a few lighters.

Some fishing vessels are tied up to the quay. Most of them also carry food and other goods to the villages situated further to the north. Upernavik is virtually the most northerly port visited by ships coming from Europe, though the base at Thule is supplied in the summer by convoys preceded by ice-breakers. The transport of goods to the north of Upernavik is very irregular, and the Eskimos in those regions have to hunt more actively than their brothers in the south in order to survive.

During his third voyage, in 1587, Davis reached Qaersorssuak Island, a little to the south of Upernavik, and he named its western extremity 'Sanderson's Hope', after one of his backers. That was the most northerly point that Davis ever recorded in his arctic log. It was not until 1616 that the sixth expedition of the *Discovery* passed Sanderson's Hope and reached a latitude of 78°N.—a record which was not broken until 1853. A Frenchman, Robert Bylot was captain of the *Discovery*; but it was the Englishman William Baffin who described the events of the voyage, and his name finally eclipsed that of Bylot. For us too, Upernavik is an important milestone on our journey. Up to now, we have only been engaged on an approach run; but that ends here, and our real difficulties are about to begin.

Amundsen, who was the first navigator to complete the North-West Passage, regarded the crossing of Melville Bay as potentially the most difficult part of the journey.

Melville Bay is a large stretch of water, extending from Holms Island in the south to Cape York, 165 miles further north. It provides a route for ships bound for the north of Baffin Bay and for Kane Basin.

In the nineteenth century, English whalers used to sail these waters, and most of the available information about the crossing comes from them. The results of my preliminary studies indicated that an ice-free zone, known as 'North Water' or 'Open Water', opens up early in the season to the north of Cape York, and stretches across Baffin Bay to Bylot Island to the south of Lancaster

Sound in the Canadian Arctic. This route was preferred by the whalers, each of whom wanted to be first in the field every season. Quite a few ships were lost in those waters, and the crossing of Melville Bay is regarded as particularly hazardous.

This crossing is difficult because of the considerable concentration of thick ice. There are many glaciers along the shores of the bay, and they give rise to a multitude of icebergs. Their total number is unknown; but Disco Island and the southern part of the Svartenhuk Peninsula are known to calve about 5,400 icebergs every year. These icebergs drift northwards on the current and join forces with the icebergs produced on the shores of Melville Bay, creating an enormous concentration of freshwater ice (which is the hardest variety), to which must be added the pack-ice created by the freezing of the sea.

Icebergs are dangerous for every kind of vessel. The American icebreaker-tanker *Manhattan*, displacing 200,000 tons and specially strengthened for a trial voyage in the North-West, had its hull holed by an iceberg, and only stayed afloat because of its watertight compartments. But the worst danger obviously is that of being caught in the ice and crushed by its pressure.

Being well aware that I have little practical experience in this field, I must be doubly careful.

Strong in this resolution, we set sail from Upernavik. The most recent ice report came in yesterday; it indicates that Melville Bay is impassable at present, but suggests that it may be possible to reach Kraulshavn, a small Eskimo settlement situated on 74° 07' N. in an indentation of the south coast of Nugssuaq Island, 80 miles to the north of Upernavik. I have drawn up a route plan on a basis of the most recent information that can be gathered from the local radio station, and intend to take the inner passage as far as Tugtorqortoq Island (Eskimo is not an easy language!). From there I shall follow a route outside the islands to Kraulshavn—in a straight line if possible.

On our way, we shall have to pass several fjords which are connected with the glaciers of the central Greenland icecap, including Upernavik Isfjord, Gieseckes Isfjord and Ussings Isfjord. Nugssuaq Island, our present destination, is itself part of the northern shore of Ryders Isfjord, which might make it very difficult to get in to Kraulshavn. Well, we shall soon know more about it than we do now!

The *Bernier* catches up with us at Upernavik, and we are able to improve our acquaintance with her crew—especially with Marie-Eve. I teach her how to make bread! As they are waiting for some spare parts to arrive by helicopter, we are the first to set out. This means that I shall be able to tell them about our experiences over the radio, and warn them of difficulties. I have not forgotten my resolution to help them.

Jean-Louis is getting acclimatised to life on board by easy stages. He is an unquestioning friend of the Eskimos, and regularly comes to their defence. As he is talking about the Eskimos he met during archaeological research at Pond Inlet in the Canadian Arctic, it is open to either of us to cut short any argument by concluding that we are probably not talking about the same kind of Eskimo. This escape clause can be frustrating at times, but it is extremely useful, and enables us to keep discussion within limits acceptable to both parties.

We have found a second subject to disagree about, besides the Eskimos—namely, hunting. Jean-Louis is devoted to the chase, and I suspect him of casting a longing eye towards the two hunting rifles which form part of my equipment. I, personally, am firmly resolved never to load them. The only concession I make to my companion is that he can maintain them. As far as he is concerned, he is keeping them ready for the hunt; as far as I am concerned he is preventing them from rusting. This keeps us both happy.

But there are plenty of subjects on which we agree. Sometimes we talk about his famous grandfather, and Jean-Louis has given me a copy of the book the explorer wrote about his expedition. Here and there I find a phrase in this work which seems to me to betray a warmth of feeling, all perfectly honourable, towards the fair sex. I share this feeling myself, and, though I cannot match his successes in this field, I am glad to find I have something in common with the great man!

Our references, always very respectful, to Adrien de Gerlache do something to relax the atmosphere, which is a little too solemn for my liking. They also allow me to learn something about the inner nature of my companion, who has a natural reserve of character which keeps him at a certain distance. He has very good manners, a little too formal perhaps for our present circumstances, and bears all the signs of having been brought up to be respectful to the establishment. He consequently never argues about the decisions taken by his elders—and I should be quite wrong to complain about that. I could wish for a little more warmth in our relationship, but the dangerous circumstances of our voyage and Jean-Louis's lack of experience at sea compel me to maintain strict discipline, of a necessarily exacting character. This overrides my natural wish to win his affection.

To sum up, our relations are good, but seem to be somewhat lacking in warmth. I hope, however, that action will bring us closer together, and I do not forget that Jean-Louis has only been on board for about a fortnight.

The magnetic compass is now scarcely attracted to the Pole, and navigation is becoming more difficult. Finding myself on the leading marks for leaving Upernavik harbour, which indicate the direction 106° True, I make a precise identification of Karrat Island, of which I must double the south-west extremity, for I am using a technique which involves observing the following rules: identify the next landmark before you leave a known position; establish the magnetic bearing of the new landmark and observe any possible changes in that bearing so as to have a precise idea from minute to minute of the compass error, thus gaining a certain amount of experience which will be useful if visibility deteriorates.

The sun is not visible at the moment, but I have precomputed its azimuth for the next few hours so that I can draw on an extra source of reference if the situation arises. In a voyage like this, two precautions are worth more than one.

It is still early morning; we weigh anchor at about 6, and the sun has not yet managed to pierce the veil of stratocumulus which covers the sky. From Karrat Island the route bends north to Nunarssuaq Island, which can be distinguished from the neighbouring Angissoq Island by taking a line from Upernavik through the western extremity of Karrat Island, the continuation of which point directly at Nunarssuaq. We then sail past several other islands, and come out into Upernavik Isfjord.

This fjord is from three to five miles wide, and leads in to the lower end of Upernavik Glacier, which has the highest rate of production in the region. The numerous icebergs which split off from this glacier cannot float out to sea because of the large number of islands in the way. For this reason, Upernavik Isfjord does not normally open up before the end of July, and we are lucky to be able to get through. There is, of course, quite a concentration of ice, and we have to zigzag between the bergs. Surrounded on all sides by floating ice which masks the horizon, I lose sight of the peak of Tugssak Island, which is our next mark, and Jean-Louis climbs the mast to look for it and give me the direction. This enables me to keep on course for a time, but then the fog comes down, and our situation suddenly becomes somewhat precarious. But luckily the fog lifts, and I have no difficulty in finding north again with the help of the peak of Tugssak Island. The clearing of the fog was not wholly a matter of luck; before going in amongst the ice I had checked my psychrometer, and I knew that the conditions for persistent fog were not present. We are pleased, however, to find easier sailing conditions after we have rounded Tugssak Island.

A few houses can be seen on this island, which has a small Eskimo settlement—forty souls in all, very isolated, alone on an insignificant patch of darkness in a sea of light . . .

For a time we make headway without difficulty, but another concentration of floating ice holds us up between the islands of Augpilagtok and Quavdlunat. A magnetic anomaly has been reported near the latter island which could have complicated things, especially since the height of the surrounding icebergs does not allow us to identify any landmarks. At the moment, however, the sun is shining in a clear sky, which guides us through the chaotic maze of ruined palaces and cathedrals. What a scene! What wonderful nuances break up the apparent uniformity of the white tones! There are bright patches of ice, moistened by the warmth of the sun's rays, which shine like mirrors; there are soft shadows, bordered by a clear-cut edge which breaks up the light into vibrant reds, violets and blues. God, it's beautiful!

We slowly pick our way forward, following a path the end of which we cannot see. Can we go on? A huge iceberg bars our way, and I have to make a long detour to get round it. At 1830, after hours of effort, I finally identify part of Quavdlunat Island, which is what we have been looking for. Then we skirt Horse Head Island on the way to Kraulshavn.

Towards midnight, slightly to the north of an island shaped like a sugar-loaf, we run into ice again. We cannot see Kraulshavn because of the ice, but we find our way into the bay and anchor opposite the village, watched by its inhabitants, who are amazed to see a sailing vessel. We are very tired, and do not sit up for long. As soon as I am in my bunk, I have a dream in which I see the central icecap weeping tears of ice into a white handkerchief which covers a pair of hands, the palms half opened and turned upwards. A corner of the handkerchief is embroidered with the initial 'M' for Melville! The dream soon becomes a nightmare.

12

In the Embrace of the Ice Queen

Kraulshavn, a small settlement founded in 1921, is an advanced supply port for the wandering hunters of the far north. At one time there were plenty of foxes, polar bears, seals and whales in the region. But the use of firearms and the European demand for furs have upset the original balance of nature, and so the fur-bearing animals have been brought near to extinction. The whales of Baffin Bay were ruthlessly hunted down as soon as European whalers had exhausted the stocks in the waters around Spitzbergen, and they too have gradually disappeared. Kraulshavn now has about one hundred inhabitants. They are visibly short of money, and a few Eskimos visit us in the hope of selling some trinket or other. Jean-Louis is interested in a set of bear's teeth which he buys after a short discussion; and I purchase a pair of sealskin boots—second-hand, because we cannot wait for a new pair to be made.

The *Bernier* has had some trouble with its reduction gear, and Captain Réal called me up on the radio and asked me to wait for him, so that we could cross Melville Bay together. They are due here this evening, and we shall be able to start tomorrow morning.

We are already asleep when the *Bernier* comes into harbour; naturally enough, we get up to welcome them. The reduction gear is making an unusual noise, showing that something is sticking inside. Réal attributes the fault to a lack of oil due to the negligence of one of his crew, but he is not worried about the rest of the voyage, because he is carrying a spare gear box. Being a trained mechanic, I naturally offer him a helping hand if necessary; but he doesn't think he needs any help at the moment.

Besides Réal, the crew of the *J. E. Bernier II* consists of Marie-Eve (photographer and second navigator), Jacques (camera-man), Pierre (ecologist) and Yves (professional seaman and officer of the watch). All of them, including the skipper, are about thirty years old. Marie-Eve seems to me—gallantry apart—to be the youngest of the five. She has made a very deep impression on me. With a very delicate sense of human relationships, she acts as a link

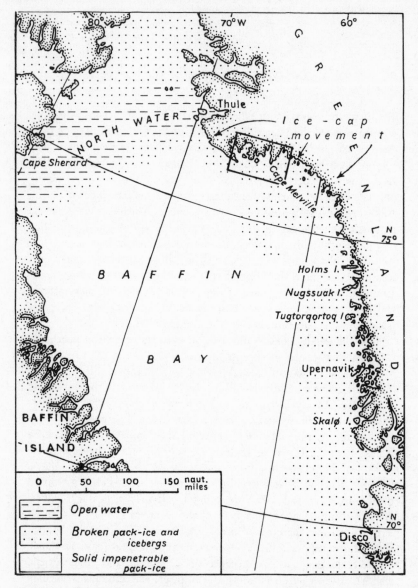

Above Melville Bay was rightly feared by the early whalers, who had to cross it to reach a stretch of open water further to the north, which was favourable to their operations.

86

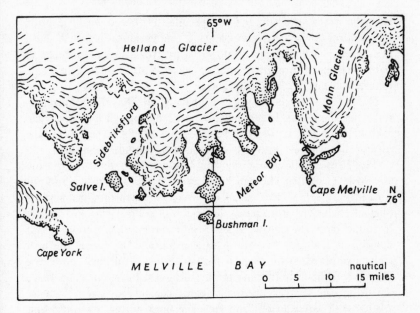

Many ships were lost in Melville Bay, crushed by the icebergs and the pack-ice. Amundsen crossed the Bay quite easily, but at about the same time the *Vega* sank, and the *Balanea* was caught in the ice for 80 days. *Williwaw*, having taken the *J. E. Bernier II* under her wing, was only able to ensure the safety of the two vessels by taking prompt and decisive action.

Above Sketch of part of Melville Bay: the Greenland ice cap stretches right down to the level of the pack-ice. Land and sea are diffiicult to distinguish in a region where both are covered with ice. Icebergs and pack-ice dispute the mastery of the Bay.

between the skipper and the rest of the crew. Jacques, Pierre and Yves are also three very nice fellows, and seem to make a good team. Réal is not so easy to sum up, and I admit that I have not yet formed any definite opinion about him. The atmosphere and efficiency of a ship are generally dependent on the skipper's personality; and I notice that Réal is less strict than myself. It is certainly too early to say any more than that. But I already feel sure that his ideas are very different from my own.

As agreed, we set sail the following morning. To begin with I remain at the helm as we pick our way among the icebergs, but later the water opens up and we are able to proceed with the automatic pilot, on a true course of 315°. The variation is 65° W., and the weather situation is as follows: wind from the north, force 3; barometer at 1013 millibars, falling; sky cloudy; rain intermittent; temperature 41°F.; visibility good.

During the afternoon, I get a bearing on Djavelens Tommel-finger on the beam. It is a conspicuous landmark. I take a vertical sextant angle which places us 22 miles due west of its summit. This means that we have entered Melville Bay. The die is cast!

The *Bernier* follows us some way behind, and from time to time we slow up so that she can keep us in sight. Towards midnight (local time), at 74° 56' N., 60° 05' W., we reach our first serious obstacle, which is an impassable stretch of solid pack-ice. I decide to round it on the landward side, for I want to know more about conditions inshore. According to the *Sailing Directions*, the best route lies between the coastal ice and the central pack-ice of the Bay. It is difficult to identify the dividing line between them. If we are to be sure that we are really in the coastal ice-zone before we try to work our way out and find the open water, we must first move in towards the coast. The ice here includes both icebergs and pack, and it becomes more and more dense so that it is soon impossible to steer a straight course.

The main obstruction comes from the pressure ridges—long walls of ice which surround flat areas like the moles of a huge harbour basin. What you have to do is to get into one of these basins and then try to get out of it into the next one without going off course. But there is frequently no way out at the right point. Then you have to try again, to return on your tracks, or to force your way through like an icebreaker. Sometimes you have to get out quickly the same way you went in—if, that is to say, the opening is still there, for the pack is constantly on the move. In this case, you have to try to go on by another route. From time to time, in places where the thaw has not yet done its work, we come up against great expanses of solid, impenetrable pack-ice.

During the morning of July 25, when we have been making our way through the bay for more than twenty-four hours, the *Bernier* suddenly seems to stop in her tracks. Tired of waiting, we make our way back to her and discover that her reduction gear, which has been running badly, has now literally disintegrated, and must be replaced at once. Jacques and Yves are going to attend to the matter. Meanwhile, I insist on taking the *Bernier* in tow. Réal does not seem keen on the idea; it offends his pride to see his vessel on a tow-rope behind *Williwaw*. But he has no choice: I have no intention of staying there for ever, and his vessel, without any means of propulsion, is in real danger. So I take them in tow for the time necessary to replace the defective reverse gear, after renewing my offer of technical help.

Zigzagging with the *Bernier* between the floes (stretches of sea-ice which do not form part of the coastal pack), I succeed in making good progress, and in the evening, when our Canadian friends let me know that the repairs have been completed, we have wasted little time.

Having cast off the tow-rope, I am confronted by two stretches of thick pack-ice which seem to converge in the distance. Between them is a long, funnel-shaped channel, which does not seem to me to have any way out at the far end. Having stopped to think the matter over, I see the *Bernier* sail by and enter the channel between the two floes. 'Ah, no!', I call out to Jean-Louis, 'Réal is not going to make us follow him in there! He may not realise it, but it's extremely dangerous!' Réal notices that we are not following him, and comes back to us. He announces that he has decided to go into the channel and break a way through. He tells me that he has equipped his vessel with a reinforced stem for this sort of operation, which is common practice in these icy waters.

I point out that I have my own capital tied up in the voyage, and that I do not want to run the risk of losing my boat—or even damaging my paintwork. This last remark provokes a sarcastic reply. Réal says that he doesn't give a damn about a bit of paint. He forgets that the voyage may last several years, without any opportunity to renew the paintwork, and that in a saline environment rust can eat into steel plate quite quickly. After a short argument, Réal finally sails into the channel and I make the mistake of following him. The *Bernier* reaches the end of the channel and rams the ice, but instead of breaking a way through, the vessel slides up over the ice and slides back again. Apart from a smear of antifouling paint, the ice looks exactly the same as before. As their efforts are of no avail, we put about and sail a short distance back. Jean-Louis and I have been on our feet for almost 36 hours, and I reckon that we should have some sleep. The *Bernier* throws out two grapnels on to the ice, and we tie up side by side at about 2000 on July 25.

I have hardly shut my eyes when I am woken up by an unfamiliar noise. I don't know what it is at first—a sort of soft grating sound, followed by a sudden vibration . . . Then I realise what it is! Three strides take me up on deck, where I am horrified to see that the open water has vanished and that we are caught in the ice. The two vessels are pressed up against each other, and are listing more and more from moment to moment.

'Oh, damn and blast!'

I wake up Jean-Louis and the crew of the *Bernier*. Marie-Eve was already up. Unfortunately there's not much we can do—it's too late. We put out fenders to try to save our hulls. Fortunately the masts of the two vessels are tilted away from each other, and the rigging does not become entangled.

I blame myself bitterly for having followed Réal. I consider that what has happened is not his fault, but mine. I knew the danger; I ought not to have let anything or anybody persuade me to sail between these floes. Two hours later, at 0100 on July 26, the pressure miraculously slackens off a little, and the *Bernier* is able to move one length astern and take up position behind *Williwaw*.

A narrow channel has formed, which leads to a small basin measuring about twenty metres square. About 200 metres of ice separate it from open water. As a first step towards liberty, we move into the basin, where Réal passes me and makes another attempt to break his way through. But the *Bernier*, with her eleven tons displacement, is not heavy enough and fails to break the ice. More serious, however, is the fact that after a few attempts the *Bernier* breaks her reverse gear. This is something of a threat to the career of the new gear assembly!

Since I've got into the soup, I'd better get out of it, even if it does mean risking my paint. So I make a first attempt, being careful to approach the ice exactly at right angles and at an adequate speed. *Williwaw* slides up on to the ice, which fortunately yields beneath her weight. One point to us!

We work through the night and a good part of the following morning, gradually acquiring the right technique: first of all the boat has to back to get up sufficient momentum, then she sets off full speed ahead, climbs up on to the ice and breaks it with her weight. The pieces of broken ice can be very bulky, and we have to prevent them getting in the way of our next run. Putting the engine astern, we pull them free with the help of a grapnel made fast to a nylon hawser, and tow them out of the way. While the hawser is taking the full strain during one of these manoeuvres, the grapnel comes loose. The elasticity of the nylon makes it snap back so hard that it strikes violently against *Williwaw*'s guard-rail, also hitting Jean-Louis's arm, though luckily he is standing far enough back from the life-line to avoid the worst of the impact. This is a warning that we must be more careful in future. We take special care to ensure that the grapnel has taken a firm hold; and we take cover against the possible snap-back when the hawser is under tension. A metal cable or chain would be free from this dangerous elasticity, but it would be too heavy for a small crew to handle.

To begin with Jean-Louis and I do the work, while Jacques' camera records our efforts. Then we agree to a division of labour. Jacques will either lend us a hand or will film the job on behalf of both expeditions; for I want to include the scene in my own film of the voyage, but cannot at the moment leave the helm of my own boat. This arrangement is concluded with the crew, for Réal, strange to say, has gone below for a sleep!

After long hours of effort, when there are only about 50 metres to go, the channel seems to become progressively narrower, and I insist that all available hands must help to clear away the broken ice, so that we can reach open water before the channel closes again. I urge them to wake up Réal, but it seems that he has given strict instructions not to be disturbed. We are losing valuable time, and very soon the channel becomes so narrow that we cannot shift the blocks of broken ice back past the hull. I have to call a halt to the work when we are only 40 metres from freedom. So near, and yet so far! We anchor the boat with grapnels at the widest part of the channel which we have opened with so much toil.

I am standing on the ice, a few metres from *Williwaw*, at the moment when the implacable embrace of the Ice Queen begins to tighten on the vessel's sides. I see the floe moving inexorably onwards, while a pressure ridge is already forming both ahead and astern of the boat, amid the characteristic grating and vibration of the ice.

A tongue of ice juts out some 50 cm (20 in) from the edge of the floe which is moving towards my hull. The ice is about 70 cm thick, and the hull is undoubtedly going to be subjected to considerable pressure impinging on a very small area. The conviction suddenly seizes me that it is scientifically impossible for the hull to survive this attack. In my mind's eye, I see *Williwaw* pierced by this battering-ram of ice and irrevocably destroyed.

I am humiliated to remember my own lack of discipline and determination, to see myself fall at the first fence without any excuse, destroying what I have achieved in the past, losing all that I possess in the present, and mortgaging my future. Failure and self-contempt make up the bitterest cup of all. The astonished face of one of my children keeps rising before me. A tear runs down her cheek . . . Then the ice touches the hull. I hear that sinister creaking again as the pressure increases, producing a ring of what looks like powdered snow around the point of contact . . .

The creaking grows progressively louder and the tremendous power of the ice comes home to me. Suddenly, like a gun going off, the tongue of ice seems to explode. Now the thrust is spread over a wider area of the hull, which rises under the pressure. It is 8 in the morning on July 26, 1977. I have not slept for 48 hours, and there is nothing further I can do to get us out of our predicament, so I decide to go to bed. Everyone is asleep on board the *Bernier*, and Jean-Louis, who has worked like a Trojan with the grapnel, is also resting. I have not seen Réal since the previous night.

During the ice-clearing operation, Yves and Jacques said something very surprising. These are their exact words:

'Once we get out of here, Willy, you had better go your own way. Don't stay with us—don't wait for the *Bernier*—or you'll only have trouble.'

I did not see how the *Bernier* could give me any trouble, and I was resolved not to let myself be lured into any further imprudent action, so I replied, quite spontaneously, that as a man and as a sailor I could not abandon them in the pack-ice, because I considered them to be in danger, even if they did not realise it themselves; I thought it my duty to stay with them until they were in safety.

'You'll be sorry, in that case, Willy . . . You go on, and don't worry about us!'

These words continue to run through my mind as I lie in my bunk. I try to understand what they mean and why they were spoken, but without success. Then unconsciousness overwhelms me.

I soon wake up again, however. I am undoubtedly the most experienced sailor present—I say this in no spirit of pride or superiority, but simply because it seems to me to be obviously true —and I therefore carry the heaviest responsibility for what happens to us. For this reason, I cannot agree to do anything to increase our common danger.

Before long I am back on my feet, pacing the ice. The pressure has relaxed, and a crack about 30 cm wide has opened up in front of the boat. I watch it for some time, but there is no perceptible change. I feel very tired and go back to bed.

13

More Difficulties in the Pack-Ice

I am woken by shouts of 'Willy, the channel's opened up . . . We're free!' It does not take long to start the engine and get under way. The time is 1500.

Towards 1630 we are well out of the ice, and stop for a little sleep. One of the *Bernier*'s crew wakes us up at about 1900— an iceberg is moving towards us, and we get under way once more. We again find ourselves threading the labyrinth of the pack-ice. Towards 1930 we are halted by a fresh obstruction, and have to open a channel through it. The grapnel comes out again. The ice is about 60 cm (2 ft) thick, which is less than yesterday. Progress is nonetheless difficult, and it is just as well that we only have a distance of 100 metres to open up. At 2205 *Williwaw* gets through to the other side. The *Bernier* enters our channel, but she too has to clear away the floating pieces of broken ice as she moves forward. At the last moment, when she is only a few metres from open water, the channel closes up again, and we have to cut a way back through the pack-ice to rejoin our Canadian friends. Shortly after 2300 both vessels are clear of the ice, and we travel on until 0100 on July 27. As the *Bernier* is some distance astern, I choose the extreme tip of a floe to moor up to, and when they catch us up, they have only to come alongside.

I can't wait to get to sleep. It is just over sixty hours since we left Kraulshavn, and Jean-Louis and I have had all too little rest. We must hope that we shall be able to catch up a little during the next few hours. Some time is saved by the fact that Marie-Eve has kept us two nice hot cups of soup, and I feel fine as I get into my bunk.

As is my habit, I spend a little time running over the principal events of the past couple of days. The results of the mistake I made when I let myself get caught in the ice are not all bad. I learned a lot from it—first of all, to discriminate better between the numerous different kinds of ice. Navigation in one-year ice, which has been formed by a single winter, is very different from navigation in ice which is several years old, the latter being not only thicker but also incomparably harder. The increase in hardness is explained by the fact that in the course of time sea-ice loses its salinity. When salt water is subjected to low temperatures, it ceases to be homogeneous, because one of its components has more resistance to freezing than the other; particles of water saturated with salt are drained off below the surface by the effect of gravity, and the surface freezes. The English have a neat saying on this subject: 'One-year-old ice is no good in the galley; two-year-old ice is all right for cooking; but only three-year-old ice will make a decent cup of tea.'

This is to say that the ice is completely free from salt after three years. It then acquires a blue tinge which makes it easy to recognise. The slower the freezing process, the less the ice retains the salt. This is why the top layer of an expanse of sea-ice is more salty than the lower layers—the freezing process is more rapid at the top, because ice is itself an insulating material.

In Melville Bay, the main obstacle so far has been pack-ice in its first year, from 60 to 90 cm thick, with a flat surface apart from the pressure ridges, each of which forms a chain of hummocks along which the ice is considerably thicker.

The experience of the past few hours has given me a better appreciation of the enormous power of the ice and the potential danger which it conceals—nothing could look more inoffensive than pack-ice under a year old. The fact that a large part of its total thickness is submerged, and therefore invisible, gives it a look of innocence, which is reinforced by its watery hues and horizontal lines. Seen for a distance, the pack-ice seems to be motionless—to be asleep, in fact—but this is a trap! Once its floes have surrounded you, it wakes up, becoming capricious, unpredictable and terrifying. Hemmed in, conquered, and overrun by the ice, the open water vanishes; if you have risked your boat in it, you had better look out!

I shall never forget this first encounter with the pack-ice, and I shall certainly keep on my toes for the future. The fact that my vessel's hull has stood up to the pressures and the buffeting of the ice is another source of satisfaction. It must be said that the stainless steel false stem has done very well indeed, and that its design has proved to be exactly right.

Jean-Louis's help has been extremely valuable. In the pack, one has to navigate by eye all the time, and to be able to call on an extra pair of arms and an extra pair of eyes is a great help. I have one final cause for satisfaction—the first time the pressure of the ice relaxed, after the two vessels had been trapped side by side, I noticed, as the *Bernier* moved away from us, that *Williwaw* had made a dent in the side of the Canadian vessel. I cannot conceal that this proof that my boat is the more solid of the two gave me real satisfaction. In life and in misfortune, everything is relative; a very small thing can be enough to cheer us up.

Here my thoughts trail off into dreams ... I am really very tired.

It must be about 6 in the morning when I wake up. I have slept like a log. Glancing out through the bubble-dome, I notice the horseshoe-shaped lifebuoy attached to our neighbour's taffrail. The yellow life-buoy, with the name *Bernier* in black, stands out against a dead white background. Strange . . . Ah no! It can't be true! It is true, though—we're caught in the ice again! Luckily we are tied up quite close to the head of the floe, and it won't be too difficult to get out if we are quick. I call across to the *Bernier* and urge them to get moving before the pressure joins the ice around us into a solid mass. What saves us is that the floe to which we are moored has had its corners somewhat blunted and that the main pressure is some way off on its flank.

'Quick, quick, you fellows!'

We cast off, and I succeed in making some progress with *Williwaw*. Soon we are held back only by a small isthmus which sticks out from the extreme tip of our floe. After a couple of good thrusts, the isthmus becomes an island, and the way is free. It is 0800 on July 27. The sky is overcast, and a fine rain saturates the atmosphere with a chilly, disagreeable humidity. The barometer shows 1010 millibars, falling slowly. The temperature stands at 37°F. There seems to be some misunderstanding at the root of our misfortunes. It was my firm belief that the *Bernier* had arranged to have someone always on watch. This is the second time that I have been proved wrong. Even at the time of our first adventure, I was sure that one or other of the five on board the *Bernier* would be on duty. Anyway, it will be better not to count on them in future. Our Canadian friends seem to have very little idea about what can happen in the pack.

1. Typical Eskimo houses at Egedesminde, by the light of the midnight sun.

2. My first encounter with the Arctic; an iceberg sighted in Davis Strait.

3. & 4. Dangerous patches between Upernavik and Kraulshavn.

As we move on, we are immediately surrounded by large ice-fields. The pack often looks completely impenetrable. When we approach the edge of the ice, however, we have so far always been able to find a crack along which we can advance. Soon after midday, we make our way into a narrow channel. Just when we are nearly through to the other side, it suddenly closes up. Caught between two stretches of pack-ice which are travelling at disturbingly different speeds, we see all our surroundings caught up in unpredictable, mysterious motion. An opening forms, to the left or to the right, but by the time I can put the helm over it has vanished again. Then another channel opens up. Straight at first, it becomes crooked, closes up and at once widens out again, and finally disappears altogether.

Only very prompt action gets us through undamaged. The last opening closes just as we clear it. I prepare to go about and help the *Bernier*, but they have found another channel and have also got through to open water.

Well! That was an extraordinarily fascinating piece of navigation. How delightful to be free of that nightmare! Travelling at different speeds, the floes seemed to be travelling in opposite directions! We were like deaf men crossing a motor-scooter track on a Bank Holiday. Not a sound to be heard, but scooters coming at you from all sides! The sky has been overcast for a long time now, and I have not been able to fix my position by sun or stars. The circle of error attached to my dead reckoning is now too great for comfort, and I try to fix my position by a series of soundings. At intervals of two miles, I get the following readings (in fathoms): 82, 76, 73, 90, 100, etc. I have a note of the heading on which we have been sailing, and I shall look for a corresponding set of soundings on the chart next time we stop.

Towards 1500 GMT the fog brings us to a halt. The sea is completely calm, and we tie up side by side. We agree to move on, conditions permitting, at midnight GMT, or 1900 local time. That leaves us nine hours to eat and sleep.

The Canadians make an attempt to get their reverse gear working again. They make some mistake—probably engaging forward and reverse gears at the same time—and the sad result is that the reduction gear breaks. This is a real catastrophe. Jacques and Yves, who are supposed to be the mechanics, have plenty of

97

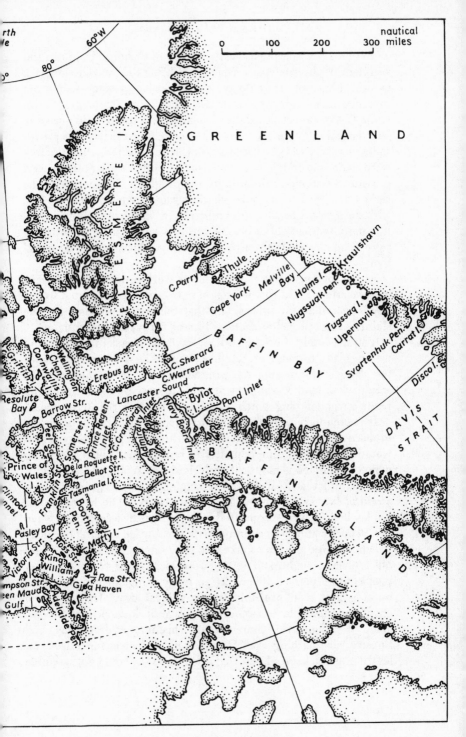

The North-West Passage.

willingness but not much else in the way of technical training; and willingness, obviously, is not enough to bring the transmission back to life. This time they do see the necessity of some help from myself, and we agree that they will strip the reduction gear down while I have a short sleep, after which we will try to build one good gear assembly out of the two broken ones. Fortunately this proves to be possible, and I succeed in completing the job. Only the forward gear is working now, but that is better than nothing, and provides a temporary solution for the problem. 'Temporary' is the right word, for I soon notice what has caused this repeated trouble with the gears. The *Bernier*'s engine has a degree of mobility, since it is mounted on rubber blocks; but it is bolted directly on to the rigid propeller shaft through the gearbox, without any universal joint!

An arrangement like that can never work properly, and I warn my two friends that this reduction gear cannot be expected to last any longer than the others, and that there is also a risk that the stainless steel propeller shaft will break through metal fatigue.

Towards midday on the 28th, everything is back in position and we are ready to move on again. I should like to warn Réal about the danger of breaking the propeller shaft; this could create a serious leak, and it would be sensible to prepare for it by getting ready a wooden plug which can be used to block the stern tube.

It is obviously unfortunate that I did not have the opportunity to discover the reason for these difficulties at Upernavik, where it would have been a simple matter to replace the rubber blocks on which the engine is mounted with rigid brackets. But I am beginning to think that Réal is really lacking in confidence, and that he is afraid of exposing his personal weaknesses. Why did he stay in his bunk when we were caught in the ice? Why is he asleep now, when the *Bernier*'s ability to continue with the voyage is being decided?

What a pity to have to take this view of our relationship! I am not foolish enough to think that I am perfect, or to expect other people to be perfect. There are so many things of which I know nothing and Réal probably knows a great deal! He may be a champion chess player, archer and downhill skier; he may be very good at chemistry, contemporary history, hydrography and forestry, or anything else. His ignorance of mechanics does not lessen him as a man. I know that my friend Guy could not assemble an injection pump; but that does not prevent me from regarding him as a very fine man and an excellent sailor. It does however seem unfortunate to me that so many of us cannot bear to appear anything but perfect. This attitude leads to mistakes, because these people end up by hiding their deficiencies from themselves and failing to take the necessary steps to put them right. Be that as it may, long years of experience have made me more than a beginner in the field of technology, and I could certainly have saved my friends on the *Bernier* a lot of worry. When Réal sheds doubt on what I tell him about the mechanical condition of his vessel, I can see clearly that he has no understanding of technically elementary matters, and that he does not want to understand them, because he is unwilling to put himself in a position of inferiority. I try to spare his feelings, and I speak to him with all possible diplomacy and tact, for I have no doubt about the danger which awaits them. If the propeller shaft breaks and slips out of the stern tube when the rudder blade happens to be pushed hard over so that it cannot get in the way, Réal and his crew are in danger of death. I should have liked to convince him of this; I should have liked him to have taken warning. Because of the work I have done on board the *Bernier*, I have again had very little sleep, two and a half hours to be exact—and it is time I slowed up. In the last 96 hours I have had about 8 hours sleep, and the first symptoms of trouble, in the form of violent cramp in the legs, warn me that I am near the end of my tether.

Réal asked me to take Jacques on board *Williwaw*, so that he film the *Bernier* amid the ice. I agreed gladly, thinking that Jacques could also give Jean-Louis a hand and let me catch up with a bit of sleep. Jacques comes on board in the afternoon, and we get under way. It is exactly 1616 on July 28.

During the morning, I was able to work out my position by dead reckoning, which puts us 60 miles from Cape York. Soundings taken in the course of the afternoon correspond with those of a bank to the south of that cape. We are now sticking to a more westerly course, and it seems to me that ice conditions are improving. Réal is in regular radio contact with the Canadian icebreakers, and frequently receives information about the position of the pack-ice. But these reports do not seem to us to correspond very closely to actual conditions. Réal tells me that there ought to be a zone of impenetrable pack-ice at the very place where we run into almost completely open water. Probably the information is not quite new, and, as the movement of the ice can be very rapid, a few days have completely changed the picture. However, Réal continues to pass the information on to me by radio, and we note on our charts the supposed outline of the central pack, for we have to round this pack on the northern side before we can reach the waters of the Canadian Arctic.

Conditions this evening have been favourable (I say 'evening' though it is still broad daylight at almost 8). The pack has been less dense, and I have been able to sleep for a few hours. At 0100 on July 29 we round Cape York. On the deck of a little yacht three men raise their glasses. We have completed the crossing of Melville Bay. Our illustrious forerunner Amundsen rounded Cape York on August 13. We are therefore a good fortnight ahead of his timetable, which is a very good omen. The champagne flows freely. I can hardly express what I feel.

The rounded, dark blue summit of the cape is fringed with snow-covered cliffs; it rises about 450 metres above the sea. This is not an outstanding altitude, and the coast reaches comparable heights both to the north and to the south. There is nothing special to make the cape stand out from its background, except for the steep, dark rock-faces which rise out of the depths of the bay, and the small granite column erected to the memory of Peary. But for us it marks the end of a chapter the details of which will always remain in our memory. The profoundly moving image of my two companions engraves itself on my mind for ever. We say very little as we clink glasses, but those few words sum up a complete epic.

'Do you remember . . . the grapnel . . .?'

My eyes moisten, my sight grows dim, and I have a momentary vision of a blue parchment, crumpled and cast aside; it is headed 'Cape York', and on it is shown our crossing of Melville Bay.

14

Across Baffin Bay

Doubling Cape York marked a useful step forward, but brought no relaxation with it. We are soon back in trouble. The weather situation this morning has little to be said for it, and it is quite cold—32°F., with a piercing, humid wind of force 4 to 5. The barometer is relatively low: steady at 995 millibars.

At about 4.30 in the morning we run into a patch of fog which hides the pack that lies ahead. Fortunately visibility soon improves. The *Bernier* is ahead this time, as Réal naturally prefers his vessel to be filmed in the leading position. To my mind, however, he is heading too far west, and the ice gets steadily thicker. Not wanting to be caught in the central pack-ice, I urge Réal, by radio, to take a more northerly course. But he believes, basing himself on reports from the icebreakers, that the ice is already passable at our present latitude; and so we remain on a westerly course for a little longer. In any case, I am firmly resolved not to run any unnecessary risks. Towards midday, I join the *Bernier*, which has been stopped by a stretch of completely solid pack-ice.

Yves is at the helm. Réal has just turned in! I persuade Yves to go about, we retrace our route. I took advantage of the short stop to make an observation which put us at 75° 18' N., 69° 00' W. My strategy is clear: to make all the distance we can to the north, and to work around to the east of any obstruction we may encounter. We shall continue with this policy until we reach the northern limit of the pack-ice which blocks the central part of Davis Strait and Baffin Bay. Only then shall we turn back towards the west.

The *Bernier* follows us close astern, for it is not easy to get out of our predicament. But I gradually manage to change from an easterly course to a more northerly one, and after 1600 our progress improves. Towards 1730 I seem to detect the outline of a ship ahead of us. We watch her zigzag through the pack-ice, and it is really difficult to work out where she is coming from and where she is going. She shows herself to us from every possible aspect, trying (like ourselves) to circumvent the pack. After a certain length of time, however, she seems to be heading south, and the distance between us narrows. I call her up on the radio, but there is no reply. We cannot see her very well, because the sun is directly behind her. She must have a very good view of us, on the other hand, and I use my Aldis lamp to tell her that I would like to speak. After several attempts, she acknowledges my message, and we try to exchange call signs; but the sun prevents me from reading hers. We steer towards each other, dodging round the floes which lie between us. Before long I identify her as the tanker *Irlando* from Copenhagen. When we get within hailing distance, I try to start a conversation with the officer of the watch, who is leaning over the rail of the bridge; but the captain invites us to come alongside, and beckons to me to come on board. The meeting is a very friendly one, and, after we have introduced ourselves, I learn that the *Irlando* has not come from the Canadian Arctic, but from the base at Thule. He shows me his route on the chart, and confirms that ice conditions are more favourable about fifteen miles further north. He had received my radio messages, and answered them. As I did not hear his reply, my receiver must be out of order. In his turn, the captain asks me about the conditions we have met in Melville Bay. After this exchange of information, we wish each other a good journey and move on.

There is a puff of black smoke and a muffled sound of propellers turning, a few arms wave and the *Irlando* continues on her way, while we rejoin the *Bernier* which has stopped a little further on.

When Jacques goes back on board the *Bernier* to fetch some more film, Marie-Eve tells me that she too would like to come across and take some photographs—but her captain quickly puts his foot down about this proposed exchange and says he would rather that Jacques should continue to officiate on board *Williwaw*. Perhaps he's right. Even when swathed in winter clothing, Marie-Eve is full of feminine charm . . . and Jean-Louis is a bachelor! (If you think that I'm a bit hypocritical in not mentioning myself, you may well be right. It isn't always the bachelors who are the most enterprising; on the contrary, it has to be admitted that their stories inspire less confidence . . . Nor have I made any promises.) Before getting under way, I record the position of our meeting with the tanker in the log-book. From floe to floe, from channel to channel, we make our way northwards, and finally reach open water—the

'North Water' of the whalers. It is 0300 on Saturday July 30, and we turn on to a direct course for Canada. At 75° 56' N., we have probably reached the most northerly point of our voyage.

I take advantage of the easier sailing conditions to check my radio receiver, and I discover that a connection has failed in the aerial circuit. This is quickly put right, and before long everything is again working normally. Towards 0600 we are coasting along the pack-ice, which can be seen four miles to the south. We have almost completely open water, apart from a small obstruction encountered at about 0720. It is freezing now, at 27°F., with a force 5 wind from the north-west, and the barometer shows 1002 millibars, falling. The wind gradually strengthens, and a heavy well—itself a sign of open water—takes us on the beam. Today, July 30, the noon observation puts us at 75° 30' N. by 72° 27' W.

A fresh wind gets up in the afternoon, and, after lowering the mizzen, we also hand the mainsail, to avoid leaving the *Bernier* too far behind. Without enough sail to steady her, the boat rolls unpleasantly. Jacques, whom I cannot transfer back to the *Bernier* in this weather, begins to be seasick. He huddles in a corner, trying to find some relief. Like so many people, he tries to find an excuse for this passing weakness. 'I haven't been eating enough,' he explains.

I know that people who are subject to seasickness are always badly affected by their first heavy swell, and I am not convinced by what he says. Whatever you do, it is very difficult to avoid seasickness. The best course is to accept the inevitable, and to reflect that seasickness is the fate of many worthy sailors, and is in fact all the more credit to them. But Jacques insists on having something to eat. I agree—though with some mental reservations, for I am quite sure, in view of his pallor, that anything he swallows will be vomited overboard within a minute. Not wanting to upset him, I advise him to go and cut himself a good slice of bread and, if necessary, to ask Jean-Louis, who has gone below, to give him something to put on it. A few minutes later, Jacques comes back on deck with a plateful of good Dutch cheese and a small piece of bread and butter. What a horrible shock!

'My cheese! . . . my cheese!'

One of my friends in Brussels has given me a splendid round of Gouda cheese as a farewell present. I started it not long ago. From time to time we have treated ourselves (and 'treat' is the right word) to a minute slice or two, always on days when we had something to celebrate. On alternate occasions, as an equally precious treat, we have had a thin slice of Parma ham, which is a present from another friend. I have been careful to avoid letting Jean-Louis handle either of them, because I have noticed that he is not very good at cutting thin slices. I have also been careful to ensure that the cut surfaces do not dry out, by covering them with aluminium foil. To sum up, I'm very protective about my ham and cheese!

And here's Jacques with a whole plateful of Gouda in his hand, chopped up anyhow, as if he had used an axe! Well, the damage is done. I turn away, and manage to avoid having a row with my companion, who would in any case not understand. Inwardly, I am very cross with Jean-Louis for telling him about the Gouda; he might at least have cut the cheese himself, in our usual economical way. Jacques stands there with great chunks of cheese in his hand, and indicates with a gesture that he is already feeling better. But a couple of minutes later he suddenly goes green, upsets the plate in the cockpit, treads on the cheese and dashes to the side to be sick. Poor Jacques is a good lad, and I obviously do not bear him any grudge for this incident; I mention it only because it shows how intimately one's scale of values is connected with one's circumstances.

For Jacques and Jean-Louis, who have only recently left civilisation and its profusion of goods behind them, cheese is just cheese —an inexpensive food, which the dairy industry produces in abundance. On the other hand I am thoroughly conscious that it will be a long time before I can replace the cheese, and it has a very different value for me. Survival can be so difficult in the isolated world of the far north that a day may easily come when I shall be glad to swap my gold watch for a small slice of Gouda. On this journey wisdom lies in economy, in all its forms. I know very well that cold and physical effort increase one's requirement of calories, but that does not mean that one should eat unlimited quantities of food. On a voyage like this, it is a great mistake to eat four slices of bread and butter when one's organism only demands two; those extra two slices may be of vital importance later on. This is a very delicate subject. It often causes offence, and is always difficult, to ask a member of the crew to eat less, to butter his bread less generously, or to be more sparing with the dried fruits or the chocolate. It is all the more difficult because a feeling of comfort and well-being is very important for morale, especially when conditions are bad; and that feeling tends to disappear when restrictions are imposed. One needs to be able to ration oneself on a voluntary basis. This is the only way the abstemious crew member can adapt himself, like the camel in the desert, to the scanty resources of his environment.

Towards midnight the wind slackens. We set more sail again, and in the morning Canada is in sight on the starboard bow. An excellent landfall! Strange to say, the *Bernier*, which has followed us like a shadow up to the present moment, abandons our route and stands off to the north. I wonder what Réal is up to. I am absolutely certain of my position, and I am navigating exactly along a route marked on the chart and confirmed by my echo-sounder. I try to contact the *Bernier* on the radio, but there is no reply, and soon afterwards I see her disappear over the horizon.

'Well damn it! And we've still got Jacques with us!'

During the afternoon we round Cape Sherard, at the entrance to Lancaster Sound, and I quickly identify Cape Warrender, which is another conspicuous landmark on our way through the Sound. We try to coast along its northern shore, but towards 1515 we are blocked by solid pack-ice which lies across our way. I have lost my freedom of manoeuvre because of Jacques; I have neither the room nor the food to keep him with me indefinitely. Cursing, I decide to heave-to near the edge of the pack and wait for the *Bernier*. I can't imagine what has possessed Réal to veer off like that, and then to keep radio silence!

Jacques points out that he has urged me on several past occasions to go on without the *Bernier*. His remark is not calculated to calm me down. If I helped the Canadians, it is because I think it my duty to do so; that is a strictly personal choice, which I regard as being entirely up to me. To my mind, the idea of leaving five people without help when they are in real danger is quite out of the question, even if helping them were to damage my prospects of completing my voyage.

One could argue about the reality of the danger—which may not be apparent to Jacques, or even to Réal. There is no doubt about it in my mind. To say more could be embarrassing, and is not necessary. It is enough to realise that the far north is not a healthy place for a sailing vessel with no auxiliary engine. The defect noted in the transmission of the *Bernier* is of such a kind that complete breakdown is inevitable before long, if indeed it has not already happened.

For a better understanding of the danger, we must remember, for example, what happened in the summer of 1903. In that year Amundsen's *Gjøa* made the crossing of Melville Bay without apparent difficulty, while the *Vega* (as I said earlier) was crushed and sank and the *Balanea* was caught in the ice for eighty days— although these two ships had very experienced crews on board. All these worries add to my fatigue, and I could have done very well without these extra anxieties. They have also created a tense atmosphere on board *Williwaw*. I'm still irritated by the cheese incident, and Réal's escapade is even more annoying.

As the boat is hove-to, I am dropping with fatigue, and want to be alone, I go to bed.

15

Lancaster Sound

It is nearly midnight when Jacques wakes me up to tell me that the *Bernier* is now in sight. He gets his things together and is ready to return to the *Bernier* as soon as Réal brings her alongside. There is a brief clash between the skipper and myself, and I bluntly tell him my views. Réal defends himself; he says that he thought I was going too far south. In that case, why didn't he give me any warning? He assures me that he did try to call me up over the radio.

As far as I am concerned, I still think that is fairly unlikely, since I repeatedly tried to contact him over the same period. The facts of the matter, I believe, are as follows: Réal is upset at having had to follow in our tracks; when he thought I had gone off course, he saw in this a fine opportunity to demonstrate his prowess as a navigator.

Be that as it may, the damage is done, and I don't want to think about it. As the northern shore is blocked, we agree to cross the Sound and to find an anchorage near the Wollaston Islands—provided that there is open water along the southern shore.

So we are on our way again. Jacques is back on board the *Bernier*, and Jean-Louis is with me. To give the *Bernier* more liberty of action, we have hoisted all sail and we are forging ahead without bothering about her. She is soon a long way astern, and we gradually lose sight of her.

We still have about thirty miles to go. The compass is very unsteady; the nearer we get to the southern shore of the Sound, the wilder it becomes. The slightest roll makes the rose spin like a top. But visibility is good, and we have identified Navy Board Inlet. This is a narrow waterway which branches off from the Sound, and the Wollaston Islands are at its mouth. We anchor in the shelter of one of the islands at about 8 in the morning. During the afternoon, the wind gets up and soon a gale is blowing. During the evening, after a short sleep, we bleed the hydraulic steering controls. The defect in the sealing of the piston noted on arrival in Greenland has suddenly got worse, and I am afraid that an air bubble in the system may make it more difficult to steer. When we have finished the job, we eat some bread and butter together. The time is nearly 2000.

Suddenly Jean-Louis informs me that he has decided not to go on with the voyage! I can hardly believe my ears. I have not been expecting this at all. It brings me face to face with a new problem, which will be difficult to overcome. It is true that our arrangement has been subject to termination by either party at any time, but I am sure that Jean-Louis is making a mistake. It does not seem to me that the reasons he produces to explain his decision have enough weight to justify it. Unfortunately it is not easy to bring this home to him without giving the impression that I am pushing my own personal interests under cover of a moral lecture—which is something I wish to avoid. Jean-Louis gives three reasons for his decision:

1. The expedition has no scientific object.
2. He thinks that it calls for a crew of at least three.
3. He regards the survival equipment as inadequate and criticises the lack of grapnels to anchor the boat in the ice.

I make him repeat his reasons, so that I can write them down and record them in the log-book.

I did not want to push him into taking up an irrevocable attitude this evening, and so I avoid argument, and merely observe to Jean-Louis that he is to be regarded as responsible for his actions, and aware of what he can or cannot do. I know that there is nothing in our agreement which compels him to go on, and I consequently shall have no objection to his leaving. I do however ask him to avoid hasty action, and to sleep on it before he takes his final decision. After this I feel the need for solitude, so I wish him good night and go aft to my cabin.

With my thoughts elsewhere, I check the position of the boat. I notice that the *Bernier* is dragging her anchor, but she is moving parallel to the coast, and is therefore not in danger. Then I write up the day's events in the log-book before going to bed—weary, exhausted and disappointed. Disappointed above all; for as far as I am concerned something irremediable has just happened. It will make no difference from that point of view whether Jean-Louis stays or goes. How did we ever reach this stage? I again run over the reasons which originally prompted me to take him on; in my mind's eye I again see him stepping out of the helicopter at Egedesminde. I go over every moment of our voyage together, trying to identify the moment when the change occurred; for I know that to begin with he was hoping to stay with me as long as possible. But nothing comes to mind which is worth dwelling on.

I try to be very critical towards myself. I do not deny that I am exacting, intransigent, perhaps even harsh, when it is a matter of reaching the goal which I have set myself. But no-one can deny that I am hardest of all towards myself. I always slice the ham even thinner for myself than for my companions!

The books I read during my preliminary studies clearly showed me that the loss of a boat is nearly always the result of a combination of circumstances, the connection between which is not apparent before the catastrophe. Small causes have big effects. How many mishaps have become irreparable disasters because of an anchor which was not ready to be dropped at the very moment when it could have saved the situation! How many others have become unavoidable because of a rag or a piece of dirt sucked up by the bilge-pump, a drop of water in the fuel, a badly insulated wire, or a half-extinguished cigarette! There are so many dangers lying in wait along the road, however much forethought one puts into the preparations. This is not a question of pessimism; a pessimist would never willingly and knowingly have come as far as this. I am convinced that it is my duty to foresee everything that is foreseeable, and that I have no right to run any risks which I could have avoided.

I do not blame myself for being intransigent about questions of safety—quite the contrary in fact. I have no right to endanger someone else's life, nor even my own—for a man's life is not his sole property so long as another person may suffer from his death. That is the reason why I gave up smoking some years ago, and also the reason why I give Jean-Louis a black look every time he lights up a cigarette. When a man has spent years in close communion with Nature and has seen her wonders, it is only logical that he should avoid doing violence to her. A smoker may declare himself devoted to the protection of Nature, and may puff away at his pipe as he makes this claim; but he is contradicting himself. People always seem to look at Nature from the outside, forgetting that they themselves are an integral part of her, and that the defence of the environment and the struggle against pollution must therefore begin from within one's self.

All in all, Jean-Louis and I are poles apart, and I really cannot see what can bring us together. I subject my convictions to a very critical scrutiny, but they seem to me to be well founded, and I would not be the same man without them. It is a pity that we did not have time for a proper exchange of views earlier on; I made the mistake of not foreseeing that it would be necessary.

It should also not be forgotten that the voyage on which we are engaged has little immediate attraction. The pleasure I derive from it is of a very personal and intimate character. The journey *could* be seen in a very different light, and that is probably how Jean-Louis does see it. For the pleasure can only reach us through subjective sensations such as fatigue, stress and the physical privations which are necessarily involved in the conditions of our voyage. Moreover, personal motivation is obviously of primary importance. In this connection it should perhaps be borne in mind that I myself, being the leader of the expedition, am sure to receive my full share of kudos if it is a success; on the other hand Jean-Louis may not be so satisfied with the role that he thinks will be allocated to him. But here I am going too fast. I have, in fact, no information on the subject; we have never been into this question at all deeply. In any case, success is still a long way off. The crossing of Melville Bay gave me fresh hope, but Jean-Louis's decision makes me doubt whether the experience inspired him with the same amount of confidence.

Here we must make some allowance for the relative meanings of words. When I say, for example, that a man who wants to undertake the North-West Passage must be ready and willing to take a long step into the unknown, it must be remembered that this phrase will have a different meaning for every reader, to the extent that the 'unknown' is different for each of them, and, moreover, constantly changes for each individual as he progresses through life.

I think that my own gift for penetrating into the unknown is something with which I was born. It has found expression on many occasions during my career as a sailor: my first night at sea, my first long voyage, my first ocean, my rounding of Cape Horn, and my circumnavigation of the world have all led me to discoveries which pushed back the frontiers of the unknowable; but I do not consider that I showed any more courage when I set out on the North-West Passage than on the evening many years ago when I calmly faced the gathering darkness of my first night far out at sea.

This is an important observation, for it illustrates the fact that the unknown is subject to continual change, while courage has a certain constant value. This shows that courage cannot be assessed directly in terms of the objective total danger of the risks one is prepared to take; it must be judged according to the vividness with which one is conscious of those risks, which is a question of personality and experience. I therefore do not consider that one has any right to reproach a man with lack of courage because he is unwilling to accept some specific risk, unless one knows all about his past history. Who, moreover, apart from a few specialists, is in a position to form a clear idea of the nature and scope of the risks inherent in our present venture?

So I shall be careful to avoid passing any judgment, since I am not in possession of the necessary information. It is also true that there could be various other reasons for Jean-Louis's departure— I have indeed just suggested some of them—apart from those he has mentioned himself, in which I do not altogether believe.

Sleep is gradually stealing over me. I feel calmer now. My retrospective examination of my relationship with Jean-Louis has not revealed any fundamental mistakes, apart from that of having accepted him without knowing more about him. On that basis, everything would probably turn out exactly the same if we could start again from the beginning. But though I can understand and excuse his reasons for leaving the expedition, he cannot be sure that he will be equally well understood when he gets back home. People may criticise him for leaving his companion without help in the face of great difficulties.

Tomorrow I shall be as diplomatic as possible, and try to get him to change his mind, while being careful not to let him think that I am begging him to stay.

As my mental tension lessens, the noise of the storm outside grows louder.

'Get up, Willy! Go and have a look!'

I drag myself out of my bunk, take a final glance at the world outside, and get out of the cold and back into my bunk, where I fall into an exhausted sleep.

16

Administrative Interlude

On August 3 we spend the whole day at the anchorage. The storm has not abated, and the *Bernier* is tugging at her chain nearly a mile away, the wind having made her drag her anchor. I speak to Réal on the radio a couple of times, and we agree to try to make headway towards Resolute Bay as soon as the storm is over. Jean-Louis has said nothing further about leaving, and since I prefer not to force the pace, we carry on as if nothing had been said. I have baked some bread, and there is an unfailing pleasure in sinking one's teeth into a good, fresh slice. There's nothing better for improving the atmosphere.

At midday on August 4 the wind drops. Well fed and well rested, we hoist sail. The barometer stands at 1018 millibars, beginning to fall again. Patches of good visibility alternate with fog banks; the temperature is 39°F. Towards 1400, the northerly wind freshens to force 4; at about 1600 it increases to force 6. A high sea is running. At 1800, we come up against the pack-ice which continues to obstruct the northern side of Lancaster Sound, and we have to turn back again towards the southern shore. During the evening, the *Bernier* establishes radio contact with the Canadian icebreaker *John A. MacDonald*, which is anchored in an inlet opening off the Sound. They inform the *Bernier* that a mine is being worked not far away, which has a machine workshop that could probably carry out the repairs needed by Réal's boat. This sounds extremely interesting, and we decide to arrange a meeting with the *John A. MacDonald*. We set course for Strathcona Sound, in Admiralty Inlet; and there, at about 1600 on August 5, I finally catch sight of the outline of the icebreaker.

We leave it to Réal to do the talking. We soon receive an invitation to come alongside the *MacDonald* for a shower. During the supper which follows, I have a long and enjoyable talk with the second officer, who is a very helpful man. He is going to organise a supply of drinking water for us, and will try to top up our fuel supplies, if he has time—the *MacDonald* is due to sail tomorrow.

The friendly atmosphere is slightly disturbed when the captain tells us that he has just received a message from the Coastguard asking him to put us ashore at once, on the ground that we have not got quarantine clearance.

I am rather surprised by this formal attitude, but I have no wish to make trouble for myself, and we set out at once for the mine landing-stage, where the captain tells us that the authorities will be waiting for us. As we come closer, I see a man standing near the quay, which is taken up by a big bulk carrier. The man, who is in plain clothes, signals to us to anchor just offshore. When we are within earshot he shouts:

'You are Willy de Roos, I imagine?'

I confirm this, rather surprised that anyone here should know my name.

'So they didn't give you my message?'

I look enquiringly at him.

'My office wrote to our Embassy in Brussels to advise you against undertaking this voyage. Didn't you know about it? I am Captain Penning of the Canadian Coastguard.'

'Yes, I did know about your letter, but it was too late to change my mind.'

Curse it, I hope they are not going to make trouble . . . it would be too stupid! Before I reached the stage of definite planning and major expenditure, I had applied through the Canadian Embassy in Brussels for permission to sail in Canadian waters, and I had received a reply that neither the Canadian Government nor the Administration of the North-West Territories saw any objection to my voyage. Much later on, the Embassy received a communication from the Coastguard service, advising them not to encourage voyages of this kind. I have a copy of the letter, which described the dangers posed by the ice, its rapid and unpredictable movements, etc. In a word it painted a sombre but realistic picture of conditions in the far north. As far as I was concerned, preparations and expenditure had gone too far for me to think of changing my mind. The people at the Embassy agreed with me in thinking that the letter had come too late to be taken into account. I have copies of my correspondence with the Embassy on board, and I am ready and determined to defend myself when, a little later on, I sit down in the cabin with Captain Penning and a representative of the Canadian Mounted Police to discuss the matter further.

The discussion soon turns into an oral examination on the subject of seamanship. This reassures me at once; I know that I have the necessary knowledge, and if that is to be the determining factor in Penning's decision, I have nothing to fear. In fact I begin to find his attitude quite helpful and farsighted. What I had feared earlier on was an arbitrary refusal. A year or two ago, a Polish yacht had been turned back by the authorities after reaching Resolute Bay, and Captain Penning quotes that case several times. On that occasion, the Canadian authorities had been represented by Penning and the Mountie who is with him now; the Captain assures me that they had good reason for making the Poles turn back, but I reflect that 'the best reason is always the reason of the stronger party'.

I discover that our meeting here, in Strathcona Sound, is accidental. Penning and the Mountie were sent here to observe the loading of the first foreign bulk carrier to visit Strathcona Sound. Sooner or later, whether here or elsewhere, we were bound to come under the vigilant eye of the 'grey eminence of the Coastguard' as we came to call him later on.

The tone of the discussion becomes progressively more relaxed, and finally we are given permission to continue our voyage, provided that we report our position every day by radio to Nordreg Canada, the Coastguard's operational centre at Frobisher Bay. What a relief!

As the *Bernier* is a Canadian vessel, I was assuming that there was no question of her being turned back. Réal tells me, however, that he has also had a visit from Captain Penning, and that they had quite a heated discussion. As it is getting late, we leave the quay area and anchor close to the *MacDonald*, hoping to fill up with water, and, if possible, to take on some fuel.

On the way the *Bernier* breaks her reduction gear for the third time, and we again take her in tow. It is a real piece of luck that she has arrived at a place where repairs can be properly carried out. Tomorrow Réal will get in contact with the mine, to see if the job can be done at once. If it can, we shall go on without the *Bernier*. Jean-Louis could have landed here, but he prefers to go on as far as Resolute Bay, where there is a better air service. He is longing to go back to Pond Inlet, a small Eskimo village not far from the Wollaston Islands where we anchored a few days ago. It is situated on the strait between Bylot Island and Baffin Island. Jean-Louis has already spent two seasons at Pond Inlet, doing archaeological research with a Belgian monk who goes there every year with that object. He is obviously drawn back to Pond Inlet by happy memories of previous visits, and that no doubt is also a factor in his decision not to continue with our present venture.

Towards midday on August 6, we tow the *Bernier* up to the quay of the mining establishment. Earlier this morning we were able to fill up with water and take on 65 gallons of fuel, generously provided by the *MacDonald*.

We stay at our anchorage for a few hours longer. The Norwegian bulk carrier, which is bound for Antwerp, and the *MacDonald* have already weighed anchor, and we are left alone in the clear, peaceful waters of this inlet, lost in the immensity of the Canadian arctic.

Towards midnight we slip away, keeping as quiet as possible so as not to wake anyone up. I let *Williwaw* drift for a while before starting up the engine, and I have plenty of time to see the *Bernier*'s red hull, with its fleur-de-lis, grow smaller in the distance. I am glad to know that our Canadian friends are safe, and I wish them all possible success. Réal has asked the Chief Engineer of the *MacDonald* for his opinion on the cause of the *Bernier*'s mechanical troubles; he of course confirmed that the engine must be fixed on rigid mountings, and I imagine that Réal now understands the position and is going to have the necessary modifications carried out.

We have been under way for some time when I notice a small envelope stuck behind the wheel. I open it, and am touched to see that it contains Marie-Eve's best wishes for a good journey. I ought to have had the courtesy to do the same for her. God! how difficult it is to ensure that one's behaviour always reflects one's ideals!

A moment or two later, I stop looking over my shoulder, and am soon once more engrossed in the problems of navigation.

17

Unhappy and Happy Landings

The sun of an arctic night tinges the high, jagged cliffs on the southern side of Strathcona Sound with an incandescent red. The northern shore is all darkness.

The colour contrast is one of warmth and cold rather than of light and shade. There can be no compromise, no understanding between the two sides, though they are separated by so small a distance; searching the narrow space between the two shores, one's glance takes in at once the dark void of nothingness and the flamboyant light of life.

No dawn has ever filled my mind with so sharp an image of our destiny as this morning landscape, in which water, ice and fire are separated without any intervening mistiness or nuance.

Our destiny . . . What will our destiny be? The question comes spontaneously to our lips, but there can be no reply. In the last resort, a man is master of nothing but his death.

'Everything is predetermined', says a voice within me, but I do not believe it. I am not a fatalist. I accept the inevitable, when I must, not as part of an all-embracing doctrine, but as an individual case, the reasons for which I try to discover. Too often fatalism only covers things which we prefer not to see or not to analyse; it also provides an excuse for surrender and for the passive attitude generally associated with those who turn to it. Fatalism is therefore not an intellectual approach which is suited to a self-sufficient way of life. It makes sense in a static society in which the underprivileged are grouped together; but as soon as life moves out of the greenhouse, and begins to flourish in the open air, fatalism becomes a debilitating and, ultimately, a mortal poison. 'All things are written'—that is perfectly true. They are written though, not in advance, but at the moment when they happen. Life sometimes gives us credit, but never cancels our debts. Mistakes, follies, flashes of inspiration . . . everything is classified, decanted, everything goes in either the credit or the debit column, and the balance a man is left with is, quite simply, himself.

And so we ourselves determine the importance, the scope and the nature of the imponderable factors we are going to have to face. At this stage we are clearly taking charge of our own destiny . . . or of a large part of it, at least. Since we are not perfect, there is always a portion which escapes us. Commonsense tells us to keep that portion as small as possible.

At about 0800 we come out into Admiralty Inlet, a fjord which branches off from Lancaster Sound and runs south for 200 miles into the heart of Baffin Island. Parry, sailing in the *Hecla*, discovered Admiralty Inlet in 1820, and J. E. Bernier, the captain of the *Arctic* explored virtually the whole length of it in September 1906, and again in 1910. A number of side-turnings branch off from Admiralty Inlet, and Strathcona Sound is one of them. During the morning we round Cape Crawford, which marks the western side of the entrance to the fjord, and we come out into the waters of Lancaster Sound. We have not yet come across any ice; I hope that this time we shall be able to reach the northern shore of the Sound, which is about fifty miles away.

In the meantime the wind has risen, and we are making good progress. With every mile covered our hopes of reaching the opposite shore rise, and late that evening we arrive at the entrance of Stratton Inlet, a small bay on the north side of the Sound. Only a few days ago there was a barrier of pack-ice here—where can it have gone?

The compass is completely useless, and we are navigating by visual observation, with the valuable help provided by the radar.

Lancaster Sound is about 500 metres deep, and the coasts are generally precipitous, which obviously restricts the use we can make of the echo-sounder. In the arctic you need to have a range of instruments, from which you can choose those which are most suited to the particular circumstances.

It is essential, I think I have already said, to keep a rigorous check on one's route, and to make use of everything that can help to determine the course. Before leaving the southern shore of Lancaster Sound, for example, I placed myself on an imaginary line connecting the south side of the entrance to Elwin Inlet (which is a branch of Admiralty Inlet) and a point two miles to the east of Cape Crawford.

Keeping on this course, I ought to reach the northern shore

opposite Stratton Inlet. As the sky is overcast and the compass is useless, I have had to rely on visual references. That is not always possible, but today it was quite easy.

The height of the northern coast of Lancaster Sound varies from 400 to 800 metres. The landscape has a certain grandeur; the hills have dome-shaped summits, and are separated, here and there, by snow-fields.

We coast along in the shadow of the hills, and I make a note in the log-book that the nights are now becoming appreciably less light. At midnight (local time) today, being August 7, the sun has a theoretical elevation of only 0° 14'. Its apparent position, allowing for refraction, would be a little higher than that—higher by slightly less than its own diameter, to be exact. But as the true horizon is hidden by the hills, we should not be able to see it, even if the sky were clear. Before long, unfortunately, dark nights and increased strain will be our lot—and will slow up our progress.

To calculate the minimum latitude at which the sun is theoretically visible for twenty-four hours out of twenty-four, all you have to do is to subtract its declination from 90°. (The declination, obviously, must be in the same sense as the latitude: north in the northern hemisphere, and south in the southern hemisphere.) At midnight tonight, for example, the declination of the sun is 16° 14' N.; 90° minus 16° 14' equals 73° 46' N., which is the minimum latitude at which the sun will not set tonight. We are at present at latitude 74° 30' N., and the margin is therefore very small.

If you subtract the observer's latitude from 90°, this gives you the minimum declination necessary for the sun to remain visible through the night; and this in turn gives you the final date of the midnight sun at a given position. In our present case, 90° minus 74° 30' equals 15° 30'; and this last figure corresponds to the declination of August 10.

We have ignored refraction in the above calculation, and this factor would in reality allow us to see the midnight sun up to August 12. This means that, at our present latitude, we still have five days to go before returning to the normal rhythm of day and night.

Towards 0100 conditions are still good, and I leave Jean-Louis at the helm and go below for some rest. I have been on my feet for twenty-four hours, and it is time to sleep. Jean-Louis will wake me up when we are passing Maxwell Bay, which is easy to identify, being about fifteen miles wide. If conditions remain good, we should be there towards 0500. So I shall have a few hours rest. It is now August 8.

Jean-Louis has woken me up, the Bay is in sight, and, despite the cold outside which makes me shiver, I am very well satisfied with the situation. I thank heaven for the absence of pack-ice. Our progress has not been held up since we left Strathcona Sound, and everything indicates that we are going to be able to reach Erebus Bay, at the opening of Wellington Channel. It is probable that Wellington Channel will have discharged part of its ice into Barrow Strait, and that we shall find more difficult conditions as we get closer to it and go on towards Resolute Bay on Cornwallis Island. But we must not look too far ahead—ice movements are highly variable, and everything can change from one hour to the next. We are, after all, not yet in Erebus Bay.

In any case, we leave Lancaster Sound behind us, and enter Barrow Strait, which continues in the same direction. It is 0713. The weather situation can be summed up as follows: wind force 5 from the west, temperature 36°F., barometer at 1019 millibars and falling, overcast sky, fine rain, visibility affected by drizzle. Erebus Bay is named after one of the unfortunate Franklin expedition's two ships, and is the place where the 129 men of the *Terror* and the *Erebus* set up their camp during the winter of 1845–46. They had left the banks of the Thames on May 19 1845, with the object of finding the North-West Passage.

Sir John Franklin was 59 years old. In 1825, he had directed the topographical survey of the Mackenzie River delta and the mouth of the Coppermine River. He accordingly knew the hazards of arctic navigation—in part at least, for general conditions are very variable—and he was able to inspire his men with the same confident spirit which he felt himself at the time of this first winter camp. The favourable situation of Erebus Bay near Wellington Channel and its great historical interest are both factors in our wish to land there, and we anchor in seven fathoms of water at 1315 on August 8, off the north-east coast of Beechey Island, which shelters the western part of the bay.

Rest is our top priority, and so we put off exploration of the site until later; and both of us sink into a much-needed sleep.

When we wake up, we lower the dinghy and land on a narrow shingle beach, the slope of which runs straight on up to a flat terrace above.

Beechey Island has in fact become a peninsula, and is connected with the much larger Devon Island by a small isthmus of gravel, which is almost entirely covered at high tide. Beechey Island rises 240 metres above sea level at its highest point, and has a number of flat surfaces at different heights, forming a series of terraces. The north-west part of the first terrace you come to after leaving the beach contains the tombs of three members of the Franklin expedition, who died during this first winter camp. Jean-Louis and I have been particularly anxious to spend a few minutes in meditation beside those graves—poor graves, hacked out of the frozen soil, swept by the wind in summer, buried by the snow in winter. Who could come to this place without offering up a prayer in tribute to these men who died so far from their loved ones? Except when I stood by the grave of my own father, I have never felt my soul so close to the other world as I do now, before these three heaps of pebbled earth, each marked by a vertically planted wooden plank, carved with the name of the dead.

'Sacred to the memory of Jno. Torrington, who departed this life Jan. 1st, A.D. 1846, on board Her Majesty's ship *Terror*, aged 20.'

The other two inscriptions are now only partly legible. One of them mentions Jno. Hartwell, aged 23, and the other W. Braine, aged 32, both from the *Erebus*.

Leaving the graves and moving on towards the place where the guardhouse once stood, we get a view of the whole bay. I imagine the *Terror* and the *Erebus* anchored down there instead of *Williwaw*, and the shore seems to be full of the coming and going of the two crews as they get the ships ready to sail. The Union Jack flies proudly over there to the right—we are now in the spring of 1846—standing out against the white snow-cap of the headland at the entrance to the bay.

Before long the men are at work around the capstans, with a song to give rhythm to their efforts:

'*Veyra, veyra, veyra, veyra,*
Wind, I see him!'

The anchors are weighed, and the *Erebus* and the *Terror* slowly vanish into the distance, towards their appointment with eternity.

And what will our destination be? I consider this question again as we mount the slope which leads to the second terrace, where a monument to Franklin and his men stands.

For me—though not for Jean-Louis, who does not intend to complete the voyage—the point of no return has been passed, and I must confront the winter and its dangers. I know that I shall do my best; if I am defeated by the cold so that one day my name and my fate are carved on an oaken plank standing by a mound of earth— let this be carved there too: that I accepted the risk in advance, in payment for my independence.

We pause briefly by the marble slab laid there by McClintock, and then return to the boat. I bake some bread before going to sleep for a further short period, and then we weigh anchor. It is 7 on the morning of August 9.

We have just spent a few hours in the past, but the pack-ice we encounter as we come out of the bay brings us irresistibly back to the present. Once again we try to make our way forward from crack to crack, from floe to floe. Tension builds up, and a painful degree of anxiety steals back into my heart, affecting my coolness and composure.

Anxiety is a danger signal. If the danger is real the feeling of anxiety is perfectly normal, and nothing should be done to change it. A man who undertakes a dangerous course of action must begin by accepting the prospect of living with anxiety. It is bad policy to avoid the feeling of anxiety by mentally minimising the danger. It is better to remain conscious of the risk and to accept the fact that one is afraid. But the ability to live with fear is not given to everybody. Generally speaking, we are afraid of being afraid and of letting the anxiety which oppresses us become apparent to ourselves or to others.

The immediate perception of a real danger may thus be supplanted by a painful secondary anxiety which makes a direct attack on one's self-confidence, and thus saps one's resistance to panic— that lamentable state in which our intelligence, which is normally our sole defence against the forces of Nature, loses its power to guide our actions.

We have in fact no alternative but to admit that we cannot measure our strength against that of the elements. On that level, we are quite simply not in the running; and so it is better to use one's intelligence to avoid full exposure to their power. In this way it will often be relatively easy to come to terms with their strength, and even perhaps to draw advantage from it. This is to repeat my previous assertion that our ability to acquire and organise information—or, to put it more generally, our intelligence—is our best practical safeguard in times of danger, and that it is of primary importance to give it full play by avoiding instinctive or unconsidered actions, and, most of all, by avoiding panic. It is difficult to analyse the elements which make up the mental condition required to resist panic. They overlap and combine with each other; they are also linked, sometimes very deeply, with the personality of the individual, which seems to be an obstacle to any rational classification.

Thus self-confidence is indispensable for the avoidance of panic; but self-confidence is based on the totality of a complex assortment of rational elements, which are perceived and integrated in a personal manner, and must thus be considered as subjective. This makes us suspect that self-mastery is no more than a way of looking at things, produced by a perception which does not correspond to reality.

At this point experience comes into the picture, for it can quickly tell us to what extent our confidence is well founded. To take one example: to retain our self-mastery we must come to terms with fear. But insensitivity to danger tends to maintain confidence to an undesirable extent; and in the long run it is probable that ignorance of peril will lead to trouble, which will sap our confidence in a more damaging manner than a realistic view of danger would have done.

Prevention is obviously better than cure, and the best policy is to acquire all the experience one can as rapidly as possible. For this reason, it is indispensable to check one's facts all the time. Experience has to be sought out; it is not a present that comes with age, but a prize to be won by method, which gives results that are quicker, more efficient, and more complete.

Every astronomical observation, for example, must be matched by a dead-reckoning position. If the two positions correlate, you gain in confidence; if they differ from each other and you find out why, you gain in experience. It follows, therefore—and this is but one example among many—that a man who does not take regular observations is denying himself the possibility of improving his knowledge. And what is true of checking one's position at sea is true in every other field as well. To check your facts in everything you do and everything you think is to my mind much more than a system, it is a way of life, and when you are confronted with unknown dangers, it is sometimes life itself!

A helicopter has been flying overhead for a short while. It circles over us a few times and lands on a floe just ahead of *Williwaw*.

Obviously they want to speak to us, and I prepare to heave-to. All three members of the helicopter's crew get out on to the ice, and as we approach one of them shouts a few words across to us, but I do not understand him. He is probably still too far away, and I continue to pick my way towards the floe where the three men have landed.

We are now within hailing distance, and I can hear the sound of the words which one of them addresses to me perfectly well, but I cannot understand the sense. I speak English relatively well yet I cannot understand a word uttered by this fellow! I face exactly towards him, but it doesn't help.

Not knowing what to do next, I ask Jean-Louis, who is in the bows, if he has understood.

'No,' says Jean-Louis, 'I don't know Dutch very well.'

'Dutch? . . . Ah! of course, that's it! He's talking Dutch!'

That clears everything up at once, and I understand perfectly. This shows how important it is to check one's facts. The possibility that I was listening to anything but English never entered my head. I received the sounds of the words spoken to me with the preconceived intention of combining them into an intelligible sentence in the tongue of Shakespeare; and, although the man was using a language which I know very well, my failure to analyse the situation critically prevented me from understanding him.

This shows how mentally tired I am. In conditions of overstrain, one's vigilance and observation are affected in a way which makes one too attached to one's preconceived ideas, which have been formed without any effort of concentration. Forewarned is forearmed, and it would really be too stupid to close one's eyes to reality. I shall do everything in my power to ensure that I do not leave Resolute Bay without having had a long sleep.

'*Hoe steld U het?*' ('How are you?')

'*Goed, en wat doet U daar?*' ('Well, thank you, and what are you doing here?')

I soon learn that the speaker is a Dutchman, who was intrigued by the presence of a yacht flying the Dutch flag in these remote waters, and decided to land his helicopter to satisfy his curiosity and find out what we were doing. After replying to his questions about our destination and our objects, I learn that he is a biologist, and compiling a list of the mammals living in the region. I hint that he can hardly have very much to put on his list, but he indignantly tells me that if we don't see many animals, our powers of observation must be at fault.

'Anyway,' he tells me, 'if you haven't seen any walruses, I can tell you that there are about thirty of them sleeping on the beach of the cove next door to Erebus Bay.'

As his base is at Resolute Bay, which is our next port of call, he invites us to visit him there. We wish each other a good journey in the usual manner, and continue on our respective ways.

This meeting has taken our minds off our immediate problems. While getting back to grips with the pack and its dangers, I continue for a short time to consider the questions of the ethics of the relationship between human beings and the animal world.

So here is a helicopter team engaged in counting the animals that live within a certain radius. Why? For the sake of pure science, or with some economic motive? The terms of reference require a census of bears, narwhals, walruses, whales, etc.; and this unfortunately shows that the primary concern is indeed a commercial one. In point of fact, it is a question of finding out how many animals of each species can still be killed without risking its extermination. For extermination obviously destroys all prospect of profit, and is regarded as primarily an error of marketing. I am deeply puzzled by the behaviour of men towards the animal world.

I carefully consider the morality which is implied by the attitude just described. I cannot agree with it. It is true that man is a predator, and I admit it; he lives on meat, and that is a fact that I cannot dispute. But to kill a walrus in order to make a pair of statuettes from his ivory, or a narwhal in order to sell his beautifully modelled tusk, or even to kill a bear for his skin, when there are plenty of alternative products available—that is quite a different matter, and I cannot believe that such actions are in harmony with the philosophy of nature.

It is difficult to take the argument any further. For me, the question is essentially one of feeling. I am not a biologist, but I have seen a whale suckling its young; I have seen the courtship dance of the albatross, and the migration of wild geese. I have played games with seals and dolphins. These were some of the best experiences of my life, and I have never felt the slightest wish to seize a rifle and transform this living fairyland into a dismal scene of slaughter. No, thank you! I have fishing tackle and firearms on board, and, if I were starving, no doubt I would become a hunter. But it would be a matter of necessity, not of pleasure.

Fog descends on us off Cape Dungeness, at the south-east tip of Cornwallis Island. The pack is relatively dense, and I am afraid of getting caught in it. Our progress is slowed up for a while, but we nevertheless manage to cover a useful distance.

Remote control of the helm, which enables you to steer from any part of the boat, is a great boon. The helmsman can stand in the bows, where he gets the best view. Zigzagging between the floes, he can make his way forward without getting caught in a blind alley. Jean-Louis is now well up to the mark, and not doing at all badly. I check our course with the instruments we have, and indicate the general direction to be followed at regular intervals. Obviously, gybing can be a problem. If we find ourselves making too many boards, we sheet in hard and use the engine.

At 1410 Cape Dungeness is on the beam, and I keep *Williwaw* between the sounding lines of 50 and 100 metres, so as to check the radar against another source of information. The fog is thick and conditions are not exactly easy. In the distance, out to sea, the pack looks impassable. It is formed of thick, hard, old ice. The pressure ridges, broken up by the last thaw, rise high above the water-level; their crooked forms give a chaotic character to the appearance of the pack in these northern channels, forming a translucent landscape, in which neutral colours are combined, in the misty softness of sunless days, with the most contorted shapes. God! how cold and desolate the pack-ice looks in the grey light which envelops it!

During the afternoon we finally drop anchor at Resolute Bay. We are very tired, partly through lack of sleep, but also because of the extraordinary mental concentration required by navigation in pack-ice; and we decide to take a rest before we do anything else. But first I have a final look round.

Sombrely clad except for a light-coloured helmet and yellow boots, a lonely figure is standing next to the van which has brought it down to the deserted shore. I look carefully at it for a moment, trying to identify the uniform, but I cannot do so. I cannot remember seeing anything like it before. Jean-Louis cannot help when I ask his opinion. We finally conclude that it must be a young policeman, and we reflect that, if he wants to ask us any questions, he only has to come on board. After which we turn in.

The following morning, with hair still unbrushed after a good night's sleep, I look out and am surprised to see that the young policeman is there again. This makes me think. Obviously, no-one is going to stay for hours and hours on a deserted beach without some good reason. And as the stranger's eyes are clearly fixed on the boat, it can hardly be doubted that the reason has something to do with us. We decide to clear the matter up, and we get ready to go on shore. The beach is about 300 metres away. I did not like to come any closer in, for the water is shallow, and one needs to have space to manoeuvre in case the bay is invaded by floating ice.

As the dinghy slides into the water, I notice that the young policeman takes a few excited steps forward. He seems very anxious to meet us!

Jean-Louis takes the oars, and I sit in the stern. As we get closer to the stranger, I can make out the details of his dress more clearly. What I took for a police uniform is nothing of the kind. The young fellow is wearing a sort of blue windcheater.

'Good heavens! He's wearing the same jacket as me . . . *And* his yellow boots . . . Why, they come from Equinoxe as well! And that lock of hair sticking out of the chic little helmet! . . . Good God! It's a woman!' Jean-Louis turns round abruptly, and the dinghy nearly capsizes.

'Go on—damn it! Row faster, my friend; somebody's waiting for us! . . .'

'May I introduce Jean-Louis de Gerlache, and myself, Willy de Roos?'

'My name is Katie Cloughley. I've been waiting for you, because I'm sure that you'd like a hot shower and a good meal. My van is here, and our house is yours.'

5. Jean-Louis studying a minor obstacle composed of floating brash, near Store Fladø Island.

6. A meeting in Barrow Strait. "Hoe steld U het?" ("How are you?").

7. Resolute Bay, Cornwallis Island. Here we make some friends.

On the way to the house, I learn that Katie and Maurice, her husband, are experienced sailors, and that they sailed round the world on their yacht *Nanouk* a few years ago.

We compare dates and discover that they made the voyage about a year before me; the world being a small place, however, we at once find that we have a host of common friends. What an amazing discovery to make at Resolute Bay, in the depths of the Arctic!

Maurice is a teacher and Katie has an administrative job. They dream of blue-water sailing, and they have come here, where the pay is good, to save up for another long voyage. They are like me, they do not regard leisure as their due until they have worked for it. I feel at once that their house really is mine. Through them we meet other friendly people, and all of them do everything they can to help us in one way or another. We are able to fill up with fuel, and Katie's van is at our disposal. This is very useful, because the air base, which has information on ice movements, is some way from the Bay—which we cannot afford to leave for long, because it has a wide opening on to Barrow Strait and is not sheltered from the pack-ice which the wind will inevitably bring with it if it blows onshore.

18

Further Progress

Two days after our arrival at Resolute Bay, the boat is technically ready to go on. But the bay is at a crossroads, and there are several possible routes to the Beaufort Sea. We now have to decide which to attempt.

One possibility is to go on from Barrow Strait into Melville Sound and then continue through Prince of Wales Strait to Amundsen Gulf. This is the route taken by the *St. Roch* on her memorable return voyage in 1944.

McClure Strait, and the route it seems to offer, are no good. No ship has ever been able to get through the barrier of old ice which blocks this strait.

There is also Amundsen's route, and its variations. The Norwegian explorer left Barrow Strait by way of Peel Sound, and went on via Franklin Strait and James Ross Strait to Queen Maud Gulf. This route, which involves rounding King William Island by the south-eastern side, has never been successfully completed since. It is the longest route on the map, and, from a technical point of view, Ross Strait, Rae Strait, Simpson Strait and the Storis Passage —all of which are shallow and tortuous waterways—are obstacles to navigation in themselves, and very difficult to negotiate when the pack-ice forces the helmsman to leave the sounded route.

It is, however, the route that we are going to have to take. The latest reports say that an impassable concentration of floating ice is obstructing the western end of Barrow Strait and the whole area of Melville Sound. Moreover, Resolute Bay itself is not sufficiently well protected to be a good place to wait for the ice to disperse— which may not happen any way. So I can only decide to try my luck on the Peel Sound route. A final visit to the air base brings me unwelcome news in the form of a telegram addressed to me personally by the Canadian Coastguard office, warning me that in their opinion conditions are not good enough for a small vessel, and that they accordingly advise me to wait.

This piece of advice really upsets me. I cannot imagine who, at

Ottawa, can form a sufficiently competent judgment of *Williwaw*'s capabilities to influence decisions which I regard as being my own responsibility. However, I cannot ignore the advice, for navigation in icy waters is never altogether safe, and it would be too stupid to expose oneself to the cry of 'We told you so!' which would undoubtedly follow the slightest mishap. So I shall have to wait here for a while. Fortunately another report comes in the following day, from a different source, which mentions open water along the coast of Peel Sound. This is my opportunity, and I must take advantage of it.

Jean-Louis still seems to me to be undecided whether to stay with me or not; he has offered to come with me as far as Cambridge Bay, which has air connections both with Montreal and with Pond Inlet, where he would like to rejoin the Belgian missionary with the archaeological interests.

Ever since I began to regard him as a bird of passage, our relationship has, paradoxically enough, become more relaxed. I do not feel the same urgent necessity to train him to a suitable navigational standard, and I am much less concerned about our little philosophical divergences.

I like having him with me, all the same, and I hope that the journey from Resolute Bay to Cambridge Bay will bring him a degree of satisfaction that will counterbalance his constitutional preference for exploration of a more structured, and hence more collective kind.

We spend a final evening with Maurice and Katie. I shall never forget the kindness which inspired their encouraging remarks and their confidence in our success.

During the meal, I find myself looking again at the big photograph hanging on the wall opposite the table. It shows four suntanned young women in bikinis, posing on the bows of a yacht anchored in a tropical landscape. All are smiling, all are enchantingly pretty; but the little one on the right has a charm which captivates me completely.

'Tell me, Katie, who is the pretty girl on the right in that photograph?'

'But can't you see, Willy? It's me, of course!'

On Saturday afternoon, August 13, at about 2, we leave Resolute Bay. The sky is grey and the cold breeze makes us turn up our collars. The compass wavers and does not return to a steady position; free from the constraints of the cardinal points, the rose has completely lost the north. We have 37 miles to cover before we reach the southern shore of Barrow Strait and the entrance to Peel Sound. The only directional indication is provided by Griffith Island, the eastern tip of which I must pass at a distance of three miles. The depth does not vary enough to be much help, and I can only rely on the radar, which enables me to identify the high limestone cliff of Cape Swansea quite rapidly. This saves me from adding unnecessarily to the length of the route, and, consequently, to its dangers. The sun is unfortunately not visible, and there is no light in the sky to indicate where it is.

The pack is relatively easy to penetrate, which is normal when the wind blows from the north; but what will it be like on the other side of Barrow Strait? Shall we be able to enter Peel Sound?

Off Griffith Island, the ice is piled up and hinders our progress. From channel to channel, from lead to lead, we twist and turn in every direction, glad that the island gives us a fixed point from which to estimate our relative position.

Towards the end of the afternoon, the sun comes through the clouds, and at once makes it easy to check our course. Shortly afterwards Somerset Island comes into sight on the port bow, and at 2045 we enter Peel Sound. Between Pressure Point (an evocative name!) and Granite Cape, which marks the end of Barrow Strait, stretches the wide expanse of Aston Bay, the southern shore of which projects towards the west, ending at the narrowest part of the Sound.

At about 2110 we encounter very dense pack-ice, and I decide to make a slight detour into the bay in order to look for a possible way through. Not too wide a detour, however, for the bay does not seem to have been properly explored, and the chart gives no indication as to its depth.

The north wind must certainly have piled up the ice against the coast in the narrows marked by Granite Cape; but as the tide is on the ebb, I presume that the water running out of the bay will have cleared the immediate neighbourhood of the cape, so that we shall be able to find some open water near the shore.

The immediate task is to get into Aston Bay, and we again have to follow a zigzag course. I am conscious of a growing tension and an anxiety proportionate to the dangers that I can see. They are real dangers, for the evening is drawing on. Last night the disc of the sun was partly hidden by the horizon, and tonight there will probably be a period of darkness. The pack-ice will not be visible; and when I cannot use my eyes, my other senses will be wide awake and under strain. My ears will listen for the grating sound characteristic of the pack, the skin of my face will be on the alert for a possible drop in temperature—and we may still collide with floating ice without any warning at all. It will no longer be possible to make any progress at night. The floes will press on the sides of the boat, whether she is anchored or allowed to drift, since they will in any case drift at a different speed. We must get clear of Granite Cape before nightfall. Here, at the entrance to the bay, we would be very vulnerable. I must hope that I have not miscalculated, and that the ebb tide will, as I expect, clear the obstruction which threatens to bring us to a permanent halt.

At about 2300 the pack begins to open up, and I breathe more freely. At first sight, it looks as if I have made the right choice; for the moment we seem to be winning!

Five minutes after midnight we reach a small island which lies off Granite Cape. The water is virtually free from ice—thank God, we can get through! The sun is below the horizon, but it is not completely dark, and we can continue on our way. At about 0800 Bear Island is on the beam.

Since the pack opened up, we have been sailing through scattered ice and progress is easy. The temperature is warmer—39°F. outside, 45°F. in the cabin.

Since we left Resolute Bay, the magnetic variation has passed from 70° W. to 20° W. A few dozen miles further on it will theoretically drop to zero, and thereafter the value will be easterly. But this information is of little practical value; in these parts, the magnetic compass is as useless as a solar topee. At 1400 on August 14, we come to the Roquette Islands, and go round the outside of this small group, after being held up for a short time by an accumulation of floating ice trapped by the islands. At about 1600 we leave Peel Sound and sail on into Franklin Strait. This is a continuation of Peel Sound, starting from the junction with Bellot Strait, which separates Somerset Island from Boothia Peninsula.

In 1858 and 1859, McClintock made several attempts to penetrate Bellot Strait from the west, but failed to do so, and spent two years caught in the ice, in the very waters where we are sailing at the moment. The thought sends a shudder down my spine!

The winding strait has high ground on both sides; in the leaden light of an overcast horizon, it looks like a mere crack in the rock wall which it divides. The sky is threatening now, the weather is deteriorating, and cloud gathers at the top of the cliffs on either side of the strait. In the distance, we can hear the growling of the pack-ice; borne along by a violent current, it crashes against the granite shores of the strait and against the floes which jam the middle of the narrow passage. The floes overlap, mount on top of each other, and grind each other to pieces. Amid the chaotic confusion of ephemeral matter, the tides calmly continue with their daily pattern of ebb and flow, asserting the permanence of the law which governs the impermanent. Dust to dust, or ice to ice—what difference does it make, at our level, where eternal renewal is the order of the day?

I have had no sleep for forty-eight hours. Not that Jean-Louis has been neglecting his duties—quite the contrary, in fact. We are often both on deck together, one studying the pack and looking out for the longest, widest lead in the most suitable direction, while the other steers the boat accordingly. At times, when conditions permit, Jean-Louis has a sleep. There is no point in both of us exhausting ourselves, and it is better to keep something in reserve.

The next place where we can reasonably take shelter is a point twenty-five miles further south, protected by the Tasmania Islands. So I must keep going for a bit longer. We may not reach our destination before nightfall, but, if conditions do not alter, we shall be able to manage with the searchlight. From our experience with the Roquette Islands, we must expect to find an ice barrier fringing the northern edge of the Tasmania group. But Shortland Channel, where I propose to anchor, probably has a tidal stream which will have dispersed part of the pack-ice; and, with a bit of luck, we shall be able to thread our way through the obstacles—provided that the wind does not get up, for in that case I would not want to sail into pack-ice unless I had to.

At 2200 we round Cape Hobson, keeping fairly close in to land. We find the same conditions that we found yesterday near

Granite Cape at the entrance to Peel Sound. This time, it is the
waters of Wrottesley Inlet which have cleared away the ice around
the cape. A quick calculation indicates that our arrival in the area
of the Tasmania Islands will coincide with low tide. As the chart
does not give any soundings in this area, we shall have to keep on
our toes, and move away from the coast as soon as possible.

At about 2230 we reach the expected barrier. Fortunately it
is made up of one-year old ice, in a relatively weathered condition,
and I do not consider that the boat is in immediate danger. It is
still necessary, however, to make our way round the floes, and I
keep an eye on both the echo-sounder and the radar while Jean-
Louis is at the helm. I try to identify the radio echo of every island,
and draw a sketch of each in turn as it appears on the screen, so
that I shall be able to know where I am with more certainty after
it gets dark.

In the end everything turns out well, and when the last light of
day is fading from the sky I have positively identified the radar
image of the entrance to Shortland Channel.

We move on slowly. The engine is running and the sails are
sheeted in. Jean-Louis is staring straight ahead, while my eyes
flicker between the radar and the echo-sounder.

Finally, at about 2330, the sound of our anchor chain running
out disturbs the ineffable peace of our haven. Thanks be to Providence, thanks be to the great Unknown who has guided us here!

We are of course exhausted, but we must prepare a hot meal
and eat it before we turn in.

Few words pass between us; there is no need for them. We are
both, obviously, relieved to have got so far. The few phrases we
utter are addressed as much to the speaker as to his companion; in
fact it makes no difference which of us speaks, for the same words
come spontaneously to both of us.

'At the Roquette Islands I thought we were finished . . . And at
the entrance to Bellot Strait, did you hear the noise? . . . That was
a nasty moment, when the bottom shelved up so fast just now, by
the little island! . . . Tomorrow we'll bake some bread . . . We'll
stay on and have a good sleep; we mustn't overdo it, and anyway
the weather's getting worse; we'd do better to watch developments
. . . What date was Amundsen here? We must still be a good week
ahead of him . . . The spaghetti's not bad, would you like some

more? . . . Well, I'm turning in; the anchor seems to be holding well, and there won't be any problems . . . Goodnight, sleep well . . . Don't forget to turn the stove off . . . What luck we've had today! We've covered 220 miles since we left Resolute Bay. Terrific!'

19

Stopped by the Pack-Ice

Up at first light on August 16, I stay on deck for a few minutes, enchanted by the peace of the anchorage. The sky is overcast, but there is no wind and the water of the little inlet where we have taken refuge is as smooth as a mirror. Some stranded floes bear witness to the shallowness of the bottom, which shelves into a sandy beach, where a miniature delta is formed by the clear waters of a stream.

Suddenly I notice a caribou browsing among the moss by the stream and quenching his thirst. I remember Slocum, who would not kill a duck in the Straits of Magellan because he did not want to destroy life in a region where it is so hard to maintain. Without detracting from the generosity of his gesture, I now have a better understanding of the deeper reasons which prompted it.

In a hostile environment, the sight of a living creature is often a reassuring experience, and I admit, for my part, that this caribou is more useful to me alive than dead. After a long period of strain, I do not want to eat his flesh, but to share his peace. And peace is what I feel, as I watch him unhurriedly munching the scanty vegetation.

Perhaps I feel a little too much personal satisfaction with this analysis of my motives; but, when one comes to think about it, there is no great harm in that. If a man who gives to the poor derives satisfaction from the gift, so much the better; that proves that he is truly charitable. Egoism is in fact a difficult thing to isolate. One cannot get rid of it altogether, and to my mind the word does not mean very much except in a given context.

At about 0700 we weigh anchor and make our way into Short-land Channel, which will take us through the miniature archipelago of the Tasmania Islands. Soon after 8 o'clock, we are through to the other side, and are agreeably surprised not to find any ice to the south of the islands.

The anchorage was a really splendid one, and we have had some relief from strain and lack of sleep. The open water is a godsend.

If only it goes on like that! This last wish is expressed without much conviction: obviously it can't go on like that, and a radio message from the *Louis St. Laurent* confirms this unequivocally:

'At a little distance south of you, 10/10ths multiyear ice. You'll never get through!'

The airbase at Resolute Bay, having had some difficulty in maintaining radio contact, put us in touch with the *Louis St. Laurent*, a Canadian icebreaker which is helping another ship—the *Baffin*, from Ottawa—in a geographical survey to the south-east of King William Island. We shall be able to report our position to Frobisher Bay (in accordance with the instructions of the Canadian Coastguard) through the *Louis St. Laurent*, which will also, on occasion, provide us with information about the state of the ice. Strange to say, the *Louis* does not seem to be receiving me well. Having called her up several times on 2182 kc/s, I got no reply until the *Baffin*, which must have been receiving me better, had passed on my message to her. In any case, every mile of progress will take us nearer to the *Louis*, and communication will become easier.

Although prospects do not seem exactly favourable, I retain my confidence. Experience has taught us not to forget that nothing changes more rapidly than ice conditions—and that ice reports, on the other hand, can remain unchanged for far too long.

For the moment, in any case, we progress without much difficulty. Pasley Bay, where the *St. Roch* passed the winter of 1941–42, is 40 miles further south. If we are held up before we get there, we shall come back and wait for better things by the little stream where I saw the caribou; if we get through, Pasley Bay may well be our next anchorage.

We make our way onwards easily enough, and during the afternoon we pass the entrance to Pasley Bay, which consists of a central expanse of water with three branches running inland towards the south, the south-east and the north-east. Several streams flow into the north-eastern branch, which is therefore probably less encumbered with ice than the others.

As we pass the bay, the water grows suddenly shallower and the bottom becomes clearly visible. I don't like that at all! The chart contains no information about depths in this area, and I am naturally afraid of running aground. Jean-Louis is on duty before the echo-sounder, giving me the essential information at regular intervals, our sails are sheeted in tight to reduce our speed. We are more than two miles from the coast, and I find it strange that the water should be so shallow. In the end the depth gradually increases and the strain fades away. Not entirely, however; for some moments the whitish reflection known as 'ice blink' has been clearly visible in the sky above the horizon, over to the right. The main body of the ice cannot be far away, and I can see that we are at present running along a strip of open water bordered by relatively dense pack-ice. There is very little wind, but the sky is covered with a uniform layer of stratus, and I am worried about the weather that may be coming. The ice blink gradually spreads across the sky straight ahead, which indicates that we are soon going to meet the main obstruction.

The coast offers no shelter except against east winds, and the next bay is 45 miles away. If a west wind were to get up, we would soon be in a difficult position.

It must be about 1900 when we come up against the pack-ice. Cape Francis is only a few miles away, and I hope that just beyond it I shall find enough open water to take us on to Kent Bay; but that is still some way off, and the look of the sky is not encouraging.

At about 2020, having made every possible attempt to round Cape Francis, we are finally brought to a halt. There is no opening in the pack at all: this is the '10/10ths multiyear ice' predicted by the radio message from the *Louis St. Laurent*.

'Curse it! Pasley Bay is 30 miles behind us . . . We surely aren't going to have to waste all that effort!'

But that is exactly what we do have to do. We have already gone about and retreated a short distance to get *Williwaw* clear and ensure that she will not be trapped by a sudden movement of the ice.

I consider the situation . . . What shall we do? A breath of cold air chills my face. No, there's no doubt about it, we must resign ourselves to the inevitable, and get out as quickly as we can, if we don't want to run the risk of finding our retreat cut off. 'Quick, Jean-Louis, we're going back!' The wind has definitely begun to blow from the west, and we are defenceless, exposed to the thrust of the ice. If only we can get back to Pasley Bay before the pack drifts right up to the coast and prevents us from reaching shelter! It is nearly 2100, and night is not far away. Snow has begun to fall, and Jean-Louis has positioned himself in the bows while I have gone to steer the boat from below, using the radar and the echo-sounder as an additional check. The wind strengthens more and more and visibility deteriorates. Jean-Louis has a great deal of difficulty in detecting the floating ice early enough to warn me about it. Radar echoes from the falling snow obscure the picture on the screen, making it very difficult to interpret. The depth is also variable, and my heart beats faster as I follow the line traced by the needle which records the profile of the bottom.

Owing to conditions similar to those in which we find ourselves now, the *St. Roch* was compelled to anchor in the bay on September 6, 1941, and did not get out again until August 1942, having been trapped in the ice for nearly a year. Perhaps the same will happen to us. Who knows? But there is only one thing we can do to improve our prospects, and that is to imitate the *St. Roch* and take shelter as quickly as possible. If the bay is blocked by ice, this will obviously be due to pressure from the pack-ice outside. Whatever happens, it will be infinitely better to undergo that pressure inside the bay rather than outside. But the most important thing to remember at the moment is that Captain Larsen of the *St. Roch*, in his report on the winter he spent in the bay, mentions that he struck a reef in the northern branch, which is the only one we can enter in present conditions. This piece of information is worth its weight in gold, and we will obviously be very careful. At 2323 we pass Cape Alexander for the second time—we originally rounded it, going the right way, at 6.18 this afternoon. The wind is blowing furiously now, chilled by the pack and full of driving snow which blinds us. In spite of the gale, the sea remains relatively calm, which shows that the pack cannot be far away. Dear God, let us get there in time!

We are under sail, and also have the engine running full out so as to achieve the maximum possible speed. Our reactions speed up to match. Whenever a piece of information, no matter how slight, reaches me from Jean-Louis, from the radar, or from the echo-sounder, I respond with a well-considered yet instantaneous action. Jean-Louis strains every nerve to keep me posted about possible obstacles ahead, and we manage to avoid the violent collision which I fear, though we have some narrow shaves. The depth of the water is very irregular, and more than once I find myself shooting to my feet to heave-to, only to see the line traced by the depth-indicator fall as suddenly as it had risen. I am deeply conscious of the great danger we are in, and of my responsibility for Jean-Louis and for all those who, for one reason or another, value our lives. Because of that responsibility I must not attempt the impossible (which would ruin everything), but get as close to the limits of the possible as I can. I feel extremely clear-headed. I have a feeling that my pupils are extraordinarily dilated, and that my ears have achieved a certain degree of selectivity, so that they only register the significant noises out of all those which are going on around us. My ability to absorb and organise information seems to have increased tenfold and my motor nerves react instantly to the least instruction from my brain. My whole being is completely concentrated on one object; to use everything at my disposal to get us out of here without hitting anything.

Since we rounded Cape Alexander, I have been following the outline of the coast on the radar. I have kept careful note of the time; and experience has taught me to judge the speed of my boat, so that I can estimate the distance we have covered quite accurately, in spite of the zigzag course imposed by the floating ice. So when an opening to the right appears on the radar, I know that it is real and not merely an illusion caused by a low-lying stretch of coast. For more safety, however, we stay outside the bay for the moment, moving slowly towards the centre of the opening. When we are sure that all is clear, we steer straight into the bay.

It is as dark as the inside of a tunnel and snowing heavily, but at least one thing is achieved: we have reached shelter. We now have to find an anchorage. Being very careful to give a wide berth to the headlands inside the bay, we finally make our way into its northern branch. The two sides of the inlet show up well on the radar screen, and if we keep half way between them we ought not to have any problems. But to begin with the water is too deep for us to be able to anchor—I have to make my way further up the inlet, though I know from the unfortunate experience of the *St. Roch* that there is an underwater obstruction there. The strain doubles and I again feel the need of rest.

I keep my eyes constantly on the echo-sounder. Jean-Louis has lowered the sails to make us fully manoeuvrable. Suddenly the bottom comes up to meet us very steeply and we back away at once.

But this is a false alarm. We search in vain for a place to anchor, but the water is too deep around the pointed submarine peak which we have discovered, and we make our way forward again at reduced speed. Suddenly the echo-sounder shows the bottom coming up to meet us again, and we have only just time to put the helm down and come to a stop. I thought we were going to scrape the bottom, but the boat just misses the obstacle. We go about and drop the anchor close by. We can see where we are when it gets light again. It is now 0215 on August 17.

I am woken by noises on deck. It is broad daylight. As usual, I express my thoughts out loud:

'Good God, there's someone there! . . . What can it be this time?'

I leap out of my bunk. Looking through the bubble-dome, I can see that several Eskimos have climbed on board. I quickly pull on a sweater and join them on deck. There are five or six of them.

'Hello!'

'Hi!'

The smallest of them speaks to me in correct English: 'Please, sir, would you mind standing there . . . No, face this way please . . . A little smile perhaps! . . . That's fine . . . Keep still, please.'

He pulls out a splendid Pentax camera from under his *parka*, and takes several snapshots.

'Thanks!'

I can't get over it. Times have really changed! . . . The Eskimos say that they are camped on the opposite shore. They saw *Williwaw* this morning, and, as they were short of sugar, they thought they might ask us for some.

They have come in their kayaks from Spencer Bay—about 200 miles to the south-east—on a hunting expedition. It has been a successful trip, and they can let us have some caribou meat.

'Done! Three kilos of sugar for a joint of venison!'

Meanwhile Jean-Louis has joined us, and we chat for a while. We tell them about the difficulties of our own voyage, but they do not seem very impressed.

'If we don't get back, they'll send the helicopter for us,' they explain.

Jean-Louis dishes out some packets of cigarettes, and I pack up the sugar for them. Before our visitors leave, I ask if I may take some photographs of them in my turn; after which they go back to their camp.

A glance is enough to show us the reef on which we nearly ran aground. It is marked by a light-coloured patch of water less than a cable's length away. Its position between two streams identifies it as being the same one which damaged the keel of the *St. Roch*. It is clear that Henry Larsen could not have avoided it. The platform from which soundings were taken on his ship was situated well aft, so that the stem could already have run aground while the man handling the sounding-line was still reporting ten fathoms of water!

I should like to mention in passing that I have a great respect for Larsen and his crew. Every bay, every channel, every strait in the western Arctic has been visited and recorded by the Canadian Mounted Police ship. A large part of my practical knowledge about the navigation of small and medium-sized vessels in northern waters comes from the experience recorded by the *St. Roch*. The reef in Pasley Bay is one example among many.

(The first collections of information about these waters were of course made by earlier explorers: Davis, Franklin, Collingwood, Bellot, McClintock, McClure, Ross, Amundsen and Sverdrupp, to mention only a few. I personally owe them a great deal; it is they who initiated me into arctic navigation.)

When the *St. Roch* spent the winter here, a member of the crew, Albert Chantrand, died of a heart attack. His grave is just on the other side of the inlet. The unfortunate sailor's last wish was to receive a *post mortem* benediction before the winter was over; and Henry Larsen made a journey lasting several weeks by dog-sledge in search of a Catholic priest to come and officiate. As well as being a very fine sailor, Larsen was a generous-hearted man.

20

Ross Strait and Gjoa Haven

Bad weather kept us at Pasley Bay until August 22. This was not a very restful period, as will be seen by some pages from the log-book which I propose to insert here.

But first of all I must mention that I have had some news of the *Bernier* through my friend Noël in Belgium and a radio ham in Montreal. They tell me that our Canadian friends left the mine at Nanisivik in Strathcona Sound a few days after us, having been able to replace the propeller-shaft and get the engine mountings put right. At the present moment they should be at Resolute Bay. In reply, I have sent them a note of our present position, our impressions of the Shortland Channel anchorage and a summary of the general conditions encountered, to help them on their way.

Circumstances have been favourable to the full use of our radio. I have maintained my regular contact with Noël, my faithful link with Belgium; and since we have been in Canadian waters, I have also been in communication with VE7ZQ, a ham in Vancouver, whose messages show a spirit of tacit comradeship, masked by an extremely practical manner. Harry uses a chronometer to ensure his own punctuality. As he never utters an unnecessary word, his messages are very short and functional. But I am not taken in by this assumed lack of warmth; I already know, from various small matters of detail, that it hides a warm heart. VE2DDR, whose name is Claire, adds the special warmth of a feminine presence. She is a cultivated woman, with excellent taste and a romantic dis-position. When reception is good, she makes it possible for me to escape from reality and dream a little. The intonation of her voice is very pleasant, and I would know her anywhere by her slight Quebec accent, with its rather sibilant 's's, and her exquisite manners. Guy is an old friend, and the only one I have actually met. He is still on holiday, and I am sorry not to be able to talk to him. But there are many other reasons why Guy is one of those who share *Williwaw* with me. For this is how I make up for my relative solitude, and my radio friends are so often in my cabin that each has a place reserved for him.

Extracts from the log-book covering our stay at Pasley Bay. (Times are shown in GMT, so six hours must be subtracted to convert to local time.)

17 August 1977
  1515   Visit from Eskimo hunters.
  1600   Change paper roll in echo-sounder.
  2300   Wind from the south! The floating ice in our inlet drifts towards us and we find ourselves in difficulty because of the reef which prevents us from retreating towards the north. Decide to get under way and anchor in the southern branch of the bay.
18 August
  0130   Anchored in southern branch of bay. South wind, force 6, barometer falling.
  1140   Wind backed east during the night, and several floes are coming straight for us. I decide to anchor on the other side, near the opposite shore.
  1715   Wind gradually backs east-north-east and our anchorage becomes uncomfortable. Floating ice pressing against the chain, and we have to keep manoeuvring to free the chain and take the strain off the anchor. Let's hope that the wind does not back west.
19 August
  1120   The wind is in the west now! The anchor has dragged in the course of the night under the thrust of floating ice bearing on the chain. To ensure safety, we must make our way towards the northern branch of the bay. West wind force 8, choppy sea, snow, very cold, freezing spray!
  1430   Anchored in the northern branch, protected by the shore.
20 August
  A day of storm! Wind blowing from west which is the worst thing that could happen for us! Can't be helped!
21 August
  0040   Hooray! Wind has veered to the east, force 7. We are no longer protected by the shore. Decide to anchor opposite.
  0615   Manoeuvre completed.

The Eskimos moved camp during the gale. I don't think they will bring us any more caribou meat. It doesn't matter—we're not hungry!

On the morning of August 22 the weather improves and seems set fair for several days. The barometer is rising, and our flag waves gently in a light breeze.

The radio of the *Louis St. Laurent* does not seem at all friendly to us, and I have to call them up several times before they bother to answer. This morning, for example, I had been calling them for at least a quarter of an hour when the Coastguard station at Resolute Bay cut in and told them I was on the air. They at once acknowledged receipt of my message, and, as I did not have to repeat my position to them, I am sure that they were receiving me distinctly. The ice report, delivered in a flat, uninterested voice, was the same as before: '10/10ths multiyear polar ice', followed by the usual comment 'You'll never get through'. My urgent question about probable future developments met with the curt reply: 'It'll get worse!' Not a sign of warmth, not a vestige of comradeship! Are they by any chance backing the *Bernier* against us?

However that may be, I have no intention of letting them influence me. We shall go and have a look at things on the spot, and come back again if we cannot go on.

'Right, let's move off . . . We've no time to waste . . . it's going to be a long day!' Shortly after 7 in the morning we get under way. Yesterday's east wind drove the ice in the bay out to sea, and it is now completely clear. After rounding Cape Alexander for the third time, we meet with floes of a different kind, partly coated with mud. Obviously, they must have been driven against the shore when the west wind was blowing—and now they are two miles out to sea. This confirms that the main pack has moved out from the coast.

Is this our big chance? Anyway, it is now clear that the decision to retrace our steps and anchor in Pasley Bay was sound. If the westerly gale had caught us outside, the pack would either have crushed us or driven us ashore. We would have had no chance of escape.

But today the situation is better. There is a light southerly wind, visibility is excellent, and, above all, conditions seem to be stable.

At about 1100, a little short of Cape Francis, the pack becomes more difficult. Once again, we have to look for leads and resign ourselves to ice striking the hull from time to time. To give the boat some respite, we move in to look for clearer water close to the shore, and the danger of running aground is again added to all the others, such as the dangers of breaking a propeller blade, of ice obstructing the inlet of the engine cooling water, of damage to the hull, of having to sail through floating ice at night, of being actually caught in the ice, and many others. Countless perils lie in wait along our route; but the worst of it is having to anticipate all of them at once.

The plan is to reach Kent Bay and anchor there for the night. That means covering another 40 miles—40 miles without anywhere to shelter! If we did not have a combination of favourable weather conditions, it would be mad to go on. A little way past Cape Francis, the route is blocked. The pack has got progressively denser, and I can see no way through. We heave-to and lower all sail. To the left, to the right and ahead of us, the pack appears to be solid and impenetrable.

I ask Jean-Louis to climb up to the cross-trees and tell me what lies ahead.

'We'll never get through, Willy! It's all white ahead.'

I was on the point of going about, bitterly disappointed, but accepting defeat as one possible outcome of the battle. But a final thought occurs to me, and no doubt it is a good reaction:

'Jean-Louis, turn right round for a moment and look astern. Tell me what the situation is behind us.'

'Well, Willy . . . to tell you the truth I can see no difference. It's as badly blocked astern as it is ahead.'

'Very well, in that case we have no choice. We have to go on at all costs!'

We creep forward, pushing against the floes, trying to make our way from one lead to another, going round obstacles when we can but sometimes breaking the ice, making progress metre by metre. Finally a blue patch appears amid the ice on the horizon, a little to the right. Is this a channel? Perhaps . . .

How long did it take us to reach our destination? One hour, two hours, four hours? I have no idea. I had no time to record anything in the log-book. The main thing is that we did get through, and,

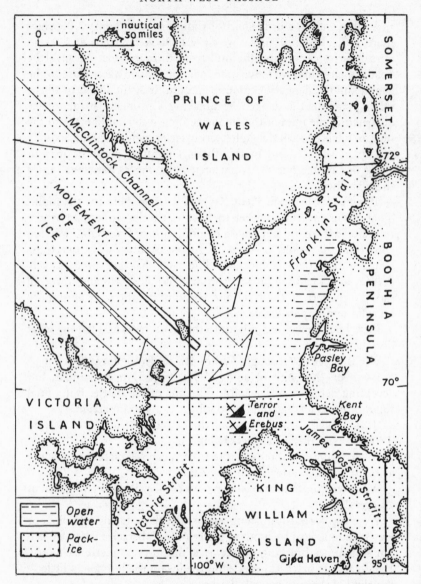

In McClintock Channel the currents are weak, and there is normally little movement of the ice, which is therefore old, thick, and crossed by many high, solid pressure ridges.

Once or twice every ten years, however, abnormal winds from the north set the ice in McClintock Channel in motion, and it migrates towards the south, where it piles up against the north-west coast of King William Island and blocks both Victoria Strait and James Ross Strait.

This happened in 1847, and caused the loss of the *Terror* and the *Erebus*, of the ill-fated Franklin expedition, which were crushed in the ice near Cape Felix, to the north-west of King William Island.

The same ice movement took place in 1977, and we had to make several attempts before we were able to force a passage through James Ross Strait, by a difficult and dangerous piece of navigation.

Position of the pack ice as indicated by CMS AIR/SHIP Fax BCST. CF-NAY., dated August 8, 1977 DTG 21.00 Z.

in the evening, after a ceaseless battle of wits with the ice, we find ourselves approaching Kent Bay. Shelter is within reach.

I can now relax a little. I am very grateful to Jean-Louis for being able to describe the state of the ice in a neutral, impartial manner, without introducing any trace of a personal reaction to the situation. It cannot have been easy for him, for that personal reaction must have been present in his mind, since the decision to be taken concerned his safety as much as mine. I do not know what that reaction was; I probably never shall, but it does not matter. The fact that he kept it to himself will always be to his credit.

'There's a shoal! Damn it, a shoal! Stop the engine! Hard a-starboard! Quick!'

We touch once, twice, not very hard, without losing way. 'It's just as well I spotted that shoal patch; it came right between two floes. Switch on the echo-sounder. I'll try to find a way further out from the coast. Let me know when the depth increases. Who would have thought of this happening? We're already three miles out!'

Williwaw slowly makes her way further out. The patch is a big one, and for several minutes, which seem like hours, we have only a few centimetres of water under the keel. In the end we gradually get back to a reasonable depth. As the tension relaxes, a terrible feeling of lassitude, produced by my recent expenditure of nervous energy, takes possession of me.

I turn south again, and take advantage of a small clear space to recover my self-control. I make myself breathe regularly, and try to block off my sense of hearing so that no external noise can confuse me. Only the sound of my slow, deep breathing reaches my brain; I have given up thinking for the moment. With eyes half-shut and muscles relaxed, I can see myself from the outside; I am no longer in the pack, but floating above it. At the end of a few minutes, a degree of peace steals into my soul.

'Right. On we go!' As soon as we touched bottom, I realised that the possibility of sheltering in Kent Bay had evaporated, and that we were condemned to spend the night outside in the pack; but I managed to prevent this information from completely penetrating my consciousness and adding a new fear to the anxiety caused by the risk of running aground. Now, after a short pause to mark the gap between what has happened and what is yet to come, I am ready to face the new situation which has arisen. Kent Bay is out of the question, for the chart contains no information about its depth, and, as we have just touched three miles offshore, it is probable that the route (if any) which leads to our proposed anchorage is also too shallow.

Since we left Pasley Bay we have suffered considerable stress from navigating in areas where there is no information about the depth of the water. There is clearly a danger, therefore, of setting up a mental association (perhaps an unconscious one) between the absence of soundings—which is a neutral circumstance in itself—and the type of strain which we have undergone several times since leaving our last anchorage. As there are going to be many occasions in the future when we shall have to navigate without complete information, it is best to avoid the development of a phobia, and for this reason I prefer at the moment to take my chance out in the pack. All the more so because the difficulties caused by shallow waters are going to crop up again—in James Ross Strait for example, where Amundsen ran aground near Matty Island.

Since the end of the afternoon, there has not been a breath of wind, and the weather has been sunny. We have been too worried to enjoy the play of reflected light over the pack. But now that the sun is setting, the scene has a strange beauty which cannot fail to move the onlooker. The sun's disc is just touching the clear horizon, and its rays strike horizontally across the pack, so that the network of ice, floating on a black sea, is tinged with red. The colours change rapidly as the sun goes down: the black sea grows blacker still, while the masses of red stand out in ever brighter contrast. A fairyland of ice and fire!

Darkness begins to gather and the display comes to an end. Night is on the way, and overtakes us near Cape Gloucester, at the entrance to James Ross Strait. We pass fairly close to the Cape to avoid a considerable concentration of pack-ice which is trapped by a reef lying along the northern coast of Matty Island. This is in fact the reef on which *Gjøa* ran aground. Amundsen had to sacrifice part of his cargo to get off again.

For some reason which I do not understand, the pack is not very dense at the entrance to the strait, where I feared it would be impenetrable. We decide to take advantage of this and to stay under way as long as conditions permit. Jean-Louis is in the bows with the searchlight, and I am below watching radar and echo-sounder. Before long the depth is down to three fathoms. I begin to worry again.

At 2137 we reach a point opposite Brunton Island; the depth is 14 fathoms, in open water. I am very tired. I need to relax and decide to anchor. As soon as I have done so, I see that I have made a mistake. We are exposed to a current of more than four knots. It is easy to imagine what will happen if the current brings floating ice with it.

'Oh, well! . . . If ice does come our way, there'll still be time to weigh anchor; meanwhile let's get a bit of sleep!'

However, I take in some chain, leaving only enough scope to hold the boat in position.

How long have I been asleep? Half an hour, three quarters of an hour? I have no idea. But I distinctly felt a bump, and a few seconds later I heard ice scraping the side. I mutter a few words:

'Lucky the ice didn't lodge itself up against the boat . . . Get up and have a look! . . . I am tired, and the floe has gone . . . Other floes will be here before long; go and look, I tell you! . . . No, No! Sleep is more important. Nothing will happen, the ice has gone . . .'

My eyes close again. Then the boat is shaken by another bump. I wait for the sound of ice grating along the hull, but it does not come.

'Get up, get up! . . . Hang on a moment the ice will float clear!'

Suddenly I hear the muffled sound of the chain dragging along the sea bottom. There's no doubt about it, the anchor is dragging!

'Get up, damn it! . . . Ahhh! . . . Here I come!'

I put on my boots and a sweater. The moon lights up the deck, and I am soon at the bow. 'Quick, start the engine! . . . If the anchor catches the chain will part!'

I run aft to start the engine and take the strain off the chain. I engage the slow forward gear. When the chain is slack and the anchor more or less straight up and down, I put the rudder hard over to port, to turn the boat at right-angles to the ice and to pull her away from it by going full speed astern. Jean-Louis turns up on deck at this point, visibly shaken by the noisy bumps he has heard in his cabin, which is further forward than mine.

'Come on! We're moving off! Get the anchor up, please. I'll use the engine to take the strain off the chain; let me know how it leads.'

The manoeuvre turns out well. Jean-Louis knows what to do now; as soon as the anchor is stowed, he goes forward to look out, while I go below again to watch the instruments.

And so we continue on our way. Fortunately the moon is illuminating the scene with her silvery rays. Amid the bright reflected lights which run along the waves, the floes appear as patches of black. All aflame yesterday evening, the ice is now almost invisible . . . If it were really to vanish! If, for a day or two at least, I could have peace of mind, freedom from fear, freedom from stress—if I could enjoy my wife's caress, my children's kiss, my mother's embrace; and recapture the tranquility of the woods at Pommeroeul and the friendship of my faithful labrador! So much of what I love is back there at home! And yet I left it all voluntarily. Everything is relative, including that caress, that kiss, and that embrace. What would they amount to if their object did not have his own personal identity? Our joys have deep foundations, and my mother's embrace would not be the same if I did not, from time to time, give her something of which to be proud.

And does that inevitably lead to an arctic expedition! Obviously not. There are a thousand and one ways in which a man can realise himself, in a thousand and one fields, and it is not necessary to climb the peaks. It is enough to make progress towards a personal ideal. It is enough to BE.

At 0255 on August 23 we reach a point off Blenky Island, which marks the end of James Ross Strait.

The night is still fine and we sail on. To avoid the current which sweeps in towards the strait, we intend to give it as wide a berth as possible, and to keep under way as long as we safely can.

We sail on into St. Roch Basin; its waters, in the light of the half moon, seem to be clear of ice.

St. Roch Basin separates King William Island from Boothia Peninsula. To the south lies Rae Strait, through which we must pass to reach Gjøa Haven, a small Eskimo settlement on the southern coast of King William Island.

Amundsen spent the winters of 1903–04 and 1904–05 there, and *Gjøa* was perfectly safe in the modest harbour which now bears her name.

At the end of a very good day, we enter Gjøa Haven, seventy-four years after Amundsen. *Williwaw* is only the second vessel ever to have penetrated to this point from the Atlantic.

It is 2105 on August 23, 1977.

21

The Crossing of Queen Maud Gulf:
Alone in the Pack

The boat is at anchor, in perfect safety. We have just got in, and I am ready for a sleep, being exhausted after so many wakeful hours. I lack the strength to bring my happiness to the surface; but it is there, and spreads through my soul as sleep drifts it away from my body. I gently sink into the comfort of semiconsciousness. The bunk is warm, the boat is motionless, and the muscles of my face relax as they have not done for a very long time. We have done what we hoped to do—we have got as far as the *Gjøa* did in the first season. We have done it with *Williwaw*'s own resources, without having compromised the future in any way, and we shall probably be able to go on further, to Cambridge Bay or perhaps to Coppermine. It's almost unbelievable. Much of my joy comes from not having let down the people who believed in me. As for the others, I have the satisfaction of proving that they were unnecessarily gloomy, though I have no final proof that they are wrong. Our first season has been an undisputable success, but there is still much to be done, and many miles to be covered, before we reach Bering Strait.

I am also pleased about Jean-Louis. Since he told me that he was leaving, soon after our arrival in Canadian waters, we have made astonishing progress, and I think he must now be convinced that success is possible. Preferring to leave him entirely free to make his own choice, I have avoided any further discussion of his departure which is still, in theory, going to take place at Cambridge Bay. It seems possible, however, that the success of this first season will prompt him to stay on board until we reach our wintering station—if, that is, we do go on beyond Cambridge Bay. In that case, we shall have taken one more step towards turning this into a joint Dutch–Belgian venture.

Finally, there is also the comforting thought that there is now good reason to hope that the money I have spent on this voyage, which I could ill afford, will not have been entirely wasted, and will quite probably be covered in part by the proceeds of the film and the newspaper articles.

Sleep gets the upper hand; my mind grows dim and my thoughts disjointed. For a moment I see the laughing faces of my children, then everything fades away and I sink into deep unconsciousness.

Jean-Louis and I are up early, and ready to go on shore. We want to take on fuel, and to find out if there are any remaining traces of *Gjøa*.

In the village we meet two Belgian monks, who come from Flanders. The older of the two Fathers tells us that, in the 25 years he has spent at Gjøa Haven, he has often tried to reach Hat Island in the Mission's motor-boat, but has never succeeded in getting so far.

According to him the approach to the island is permanently blocked by pack-ice, and he doubts whether we shall be able to get through. This obviously gives me something to think about, though the Father's experience does not seem to me to be very profound, even if he has often been out in these waters. I admit the possibility of an extra difficulty, but do not let it undermine my confidence.

There is hardly any trace of Amundsen's two winters here. There is just a slab of marble (now a tombstone) which is supposed to have served as a base for the instruments used by the crew of *Gjøa* in the study of terrestrial magnetism, which was the object of their long stay here.

The Hudson's Bay Company's store is well stocked, and its salesmen are persuasive. They actually do sell refrigerators to the Eskimos! They have many other products which can scarcely be described as basic—crackling breakfast cereals and slimming yoghurts, and the equally popular lemon soaps, biological detergents, trusses and indispensable deodorants. There is a striking difference between the Greenland and the Canadian Eskimo. The former, apart from his professional activities, has remained very faithful to his traditions; the latter has lost practically all his traditions, and has not acquired a profession because of the lack of industry in the Canadian North-West. Left without any occupation because of the financial help lavished on him by the Government, he has succumbed to the worst of all calamities—boredom.

During the afternoon we fill up with fuel. We still have a fair amount, but, since it remains possible that we may have to spend the winter in the Arctic, it is better to have the tanks completely full. Otherwise everything now seems to be in order, except for the hydraulic steering-gear, which is still losing pressure to some extent, and the radar, which has recently been showing signs of breaking down.

After supper, Jean-Louis says he would like to go ashore, but I prefer to rest, and he goes off by himself.

During the night he wakes me up:

'Willy! Willy! I'd like to talk to you.

'O.K.—I'm listening.'

'Willy, I've the chance of a flight back to Resolute Bay.'

No comment.

'The 'plane arrived this afternoon. The pilot is by himself, and he's offered me a free passage. He's leaving this morning at 6 o'clock.'

'Very well, Jean-Louis, it's up to you. You are old enough to know what you're doing. If you'd like me to get up and have a proper talk about it, I will.'

'No point. You know, this flight is an extraordinary bit of luck for me. I shall be able to go to Pond Inlet and help the Belgian Father with his dig.'

'Well, as I said, it's up to you. As far as I'm concerned, I've no objections. I'll take you ashore whenever you like.'

Silence.

'On second thoughts, Willy, I won't leave you on your own. I'll stay with you as far as Cambridge Bay.'

'O.K. I'm glad that's your decision—more like you. Let's forget about it. Goodnight!'

'Goodnight, Willy.'

A feeling of lassitude possesses me for a moment. Then I go back to sleep. Later in the night I have to get up for a call of nature, and notice a light on forward. I go to see what it is, and find Jean-Louis already dressed and packing his bags.

'I've changed my mind; I'm going after all.'

'Very well; when do you want to be ashore?'

'At 6 o'clock.'

'All right—I'll be up.'

It was a short, clear, precise dialogue. I don't understand, though. I wasn't expecting *that*.

Shortly before 6, I row silently in towards the shore. Jean-Louis is sitting in the stern, facing me. His wish to go to Pond Inlet doubtless seems to him a sufficient explanation for his departure; but I am not convinced by the reason given, and his real motives remain a mystery to me.

No, I definitely don't get it. I hope that these last few minutes together will bring some final enlightenment. But nothing is said. We reach the shore, and I realise that I shall never know.

Then my attention wanders and I stop thinking about Jean-Louis; I scarcely hear the good wishes for a successful journey which he utters at the moment when a final handshake seals our parting.

My thoughts are already elsewhere as I mechanically row back to *Williwaw*.

Alone again! It is a bitter blow, but I am not prepared to give in. So it's going to be more difficult from now on? Never mind!—I'll see it through. And meanwhile, there's no time to lose.

Furious, I get the boat ready for sea at once. At 7, less than an hour after Jean-Louis's departure, my faithful *Williwaw* and I set out on the leading line which will take us out of Gjøa Haven. According to the normal seasonal ice conditions for the second half of August shown in the *Oceanographic Atlas of the Polar Seas*, I should have the benefit of considerable stretches of open water in Queen Maud Gulf, Coronation Gulf and part of Amundsen Gulf, though solid pack-ice will probably reappear in the Beaufort Sea, mainly to the west of the Mackenzie Delta. So I can hope for a certain amount of respite from the ice. It is only at the entrance of Queen Maud Gulf, near Hat Island and Requisite Channel, that an average concentration of 1/10th to 5/10ths is predicted. This is the obstacle against which the missionary warned me. But the immediate difficulty is of another kind. The water is much shallower after you leave Gjøa Haven, and I shall have to use a variety of channels, which have reefs in them. There will be no help from the compass, and this kind of navigation requires constant attention, and, of course, excellent planning.

Simpson Strait, which lies between Adelaide Peninsula and the southern coast of King William Island, poses the first problem. This strait is 53 miles long, and runs from Booth Point (12 miles from Gjøa Haven) to Queen Maud Gulf.

It was discovered in 1839 by Dease and Simpson, two employees of the Hudson's Bay Company who had been commissioned to survey the coasts of this part of the Arctic.

I have the *Pilot* and the detailed chart of the strait with me at the wheel, so that everything I need is within reach. Fortunately the weather is fine and the wind light. These are ideal conditions in which to set out, and I am really very lucky.

My morale is unaffected. I am not put off by difficulties. Up to the arrival of Jean-Louis, I had always in any case intended to make the journey single-handed. Without wishing to belittle my companion, it is also true that his presence imposed certain constraints on me, and it is not all bad to be back on my own.

We enter Simpson Strait shortly after 0900, and we pass Ross Point at 1045.

I regularly compare the compass readings with those on the chart, to see how much faith can be placed in the former. But the compass is still too unstable to be any use.

After Ross Point, the route leaves the coastline, which curves away to form the large expanse of Douglas Bay. Later, with Ristvedt Island on the beam, we come to the narrow and winding part of the strait. I identify the transits without difficulty, and, as the weather is fine and visibility is good, we continue on our way without incident. The route lies through beautiful scenery, and, though it requires constant concentration, there are no major problems.

Towards 1600 I anchor in McClintock Bay, on the south coast of King William Island. I have not left the helm since this morning, and my stomach is complaining. Before setting out tomorrow, I shall make myself a snack to eat during the day.

As soon as I have handed the sails, I begin to knead some dough, which I shall leave to rise while I am cooking my supper. I am going to have to adapt my eating habits to my solitary state. As long as the instability of the compass prevents me from using the automatic steering, my diet will be based on a big breakfast and a big evening meal.

During the day, when I shall be at the helm, I shall eat sandwiches prepared in advance, and possibly a cup of soup from a thermos. Good organisation can do wonders. The bread I make on board is generally wholemeal, sometimes a little lighter and sometimes a little darker, for the sake of variety.

While sailing round the world, I got into the habit of cooking a special raisin bread on Sundays, of the kind known as *cramique* in Belgium. This custom has its good points, but I cannot follow it now because I have no eggs.

For supper this evening, I cook *spaghetti bolognese*. The sauce is made from corned beef and fresh onions, with the addition of tomato purée. I bought the onions in England before I sailed, and they are still in very good condition. I have enough left to last me for some time.

After supper I wash up and move back into the forward cabin, which I had given up to Jean-Louis; at the same time, I bake the bread. I am happily convinced that there is no such thing as a minor chore. Washing up, cleaning, putting things away in the right place, and, in short, every kind of domestic task are just as important as navigation itself with all its intellectual and technical involvements.

Our organised society has made a mistake in devaluing certain kinds of manual work. A road-sweeper, for example, is just as indispensable to the community as a doctor. This obviously does not mean that they should be paid the same. Far from it. A man can become a road-sweeper much more quickly and easily than he can become a doctor, and it is therefore logical that there should be a difference of salary. The quality of the work is not the same, but both men's labours deserve equal recognition, because they are equally useful.

The anchorage is calm and well protected. I can look forward to a restful night. To tell the truth, I am very tired, and one night is not going to make up the back-log of sleep; but it is something, all the same.

The anchorage lives up to expectations, and I have a good night. I get up early to prepare my breakfast and my midday snack. It is pleasant in the cabin; its woodwork creates a rustic atmosphere, which is heightened by the noise of the kettle singing on the stove. I miss the smell of the coffee I used to make for my companion . . . Jean-Louis was very fond of his 'spot of coffee': but I personally prefer to avoid stimulants, especially now that I am alone. When one has to live for a long time at the limit of one's capacity, there is no point in using stimulant drugs or medicines, the action of which is always followed by a depressive stage. This prevents one's full potential from being constantly available. Besides, it is best to see oneself as one really is. A glass of spirits, for example, might give you the illusion of being able to do what is really beyond your powers, and lead to dangerous risks.

My chosen drink is made by stirring honey into hot water. The flavour is not too good, but what does that matter? Apart from the glucose which it contains, honey stimulates the muscles of the intestines, and this makes it effective against constipation.

For my snack, I have just cut myself some Parma ham. It is extraordinarily good. The friend who gave it to me probably has no idea what a good present it was. Ham can be eaten on its own, or be served with various dishes: salads, *paupiettes*, omelettes, macaroni, etc. Vilhjalmur Stefansson can praise seal fat as much as he likes—I prefer Parma ham!

In present circumstances, I have to complete my study of the route before setting out in the morning, and this brings me back to navigation.

McClintock Bay, where we are sheltering at the moment, is situated at the far end of Simpson Strait, which opens out, a little further on, into Queen Maud Gulf. The entrance to the gulf is obstructed by reefs, and as the chart contains no information about depths, apart from those of the channel known as 'Storis Passage', I have no choice but to use that channel, which leads on past the famous Hat Island into Requisite Channel, which lies between Hat Island and the big reef bordering on the Nordenskiold Islands.

It is 0647 when we leave the bay. It is after dawn, but the sky is overcast. This is a setback, for I am certainly going to need the sun to guide me.

The gulf is wide, and there are no visible landmarks for a distance of about 30 miles after Cape John Herschel. The radar has lost much of its effectiveness, and I doubt if it is going to be very useful. The few islands which could serve as points of reference are low-lying, which means they can be picked out with the naked eye almost as quickly as by radar.

The first few hours of the day's journey pass without important incident; but later I notice a trail of white on the horizon due ahead. As we sail on, I have to admit the evidence of my eyes. At 1000, the pack is there to meet us.

The ice is of the same type as that we met in James Ross Strait

8. Iceberg calved by a glacier to the north of Upernavik. Four-fifths of its volume is below the surface.

9. The Eskimos at Pasley Bay.

10. At Gjøa Haven - the exact spot where Amundsen wintered.

11. The entrance to James Ross Strait. As the sun goes down, the scene has a strange beauty which cannot fail to move the onlooker.

—thick, several years old, and hard as rock. At first it is fairly open, but it soon closes up, and I have to zigzag between the floes. Before each change of direction I make a note of a cloud, a grey patch in the sky, or the shape of an unusual floe in the distance to help me get back on course. It is all too easy to lose one's bearings!

Suddenly fog comes down, and the old feeling of anxiety surfaces again. I have to hand all sail, and for about an hour I am in a bad way. The time comes when I would like to go back the way I came, but I no longer have a clear idea of the heading, and I decide not to make things worse by losing idea of my position, which is what would happen if I sailed off at random. It is better to stay where we are, and wait for clearer weather. In the end visibility slowly improves, while the sky is totally covered by stratocumulus.

I look vainly for the sun; the sky is totally overcast, and there is no way of even guessing its position. To stabilise the boat as far as possible, I drive her into a space between two floes. They protect her from the slight swell, and, in these conditions, I try to draw some sort of conclusion from the movements of the compass.

With no list and completely calm water, the compass card ought to be able to find a satisfactory point of equilibrium and give me a relatively trustworthy direction. I repeatedly attract the card away from its point of equilibrium by moving a metal object round the compass, and observe that every time the card returns to approximately the same point; finally I am satisfied that I can now deduce a definite direction from the indications provided by the compass. I pick out a point on the horizon to represent my supposed heading, and start the engine again under power. About noon, just as I was beginning to be seriously worried, I sight an island which I identify as Kirkwall Island. I am too far south. But that is not too serious, provided that I have not made a mistake and that it really is the island I think! Anyway, I shall soon know, because there is another island five miles beyond Kirkwall Island, and I should soon see it. Shortly afterwards, all doubt is removed—we *are* on the right route. The pack is still dense—5/10ths to 6/10ths of multiyear ice.

Towards the end of the afternoon, the outline of Hat Island appears to the left, and we enter Requisite Channel, which curves away to the south. It is time I thought about an anchorage for the night. There is not much choice. Only the reef which borders the southern edge of the Nordenskiold Islands lies near my route. A racon beacon-buoy marks an island near the anchorage, which I ought to be able to find without difficulty, even if night comes down before I reach it. The pack becomes progressively less dense as I make my way along Requisite Channel. I have left Hat Island behind me, and with it the warnings of the worthy missionary at Gjøa Haven!

The reef and some of the low-lying islands of the little group finally come into sight. Floating ice, driven by the south-west wind, has grounded along the edge of the formation, which is consequently easy to pick out.

Glad to see the end of the day, I finally bring *Williwaw* to rest in twelve fathoms of water, at the spot marked with a small anchor on the chart. I am pleased to have got so far. The period of uncertainty about our course has exhausted me mentally, and I shall not stay up a moment longer than it takes me to eat my supper and put things away.

During the night, the wind shifts to the north-west, and strengthens rapidly. The boat is sheltered by the reef, and conditions remain comfortable. To be on the safe side, however, I get up and pay out a little more chain.

Shortly after 0100 I am woken up by something bumping violently against the hull; this is followed by the characteristic grating sound of a floe travelling along the side of the boat. Probably one of the stranded floes has been refloated by the high tide, and the wind is now blowing it away from the reef.

Before I can get back to sleep, another crash shakes the boat.

'Curse it! They're going to hole us in a minute!'

From inside the boat the noise sounds really alarming, and if I did not know how solidly constructed *Williwaw* is I should be seriously worried.

I am getting ready to go on deck and have a look when a fresh impact makes me start. Really frightened this time, I leap across the cabin.

'Quickly, damn it! Something's going to break!'

I go forward and the light of the waxing moon shows me several large floes lodged against the stem. The bowsprit is stuck into a cavity in one of them. The bobstay is strained almost to breaking-point, and so is the anchor chain.

'Quick! The engine!'

I start up, and creep very slowly forward. I can clearly hear the creaking of the backstay, which is affected by the tremendous strain on the bobstay.

In a while the ice begins to give way before the thrust of the boat. When I have advanced so far that the anchor chain is taut behind the boat, I go full speed astern, taking advantage of the inertia of the floes to pull the bowsprit free. The manoeuvre works out well, and we turn away to port to avoid the ice as it drifts back.

Poor Jean-Louis! I thought I was giving him the more comfortable cabin, next to the stove. I now realise that he has been living inside a drum on which the ice has been playing a tattoo. Why didn't he complain? . . . I ought to have realised what was going on during that night in James Ross Strait, when conditions were very much as they are now. He came up on deck, obviously alarmed, and said that the noise down below was intolerable. I did not realise that it was really like this, and he probably did not feel sure enough of himself to say any more. What a pity!

It is a rough night. Having to be constantly at the helm, I do not get any more sleep. I wait impatiently for dawn to come; I want to get away from here. Tomorrow I shall try to reach Jenny Lind Bay, a good anchorage on the island of the same name.

When under heavy mental stress, it is wise to divert one's thoughts towards a more peaceful subject. The tension must be relaxed.

Towards 0745 on Saturday August 27, we are again under way. The wind has eased a little and is now a steady force 5, blowing from the north-west. The winch broke down while I was raising the C.Q.R. anchor. Fortunately it was nearly up, and I only had to bring it in a short way by hand. I hope I can repair the winch; raising the anchor by hand is a long job, which I must admit is beyond my strength in a high wind or from a great depth.

Once clear of the reef, I set course for Jenny Lind Island, about 25 miles away. The route is fortunately free from danger, this part of Queen Maud Gulf being considerably deeper. I am glad that this is going to be a short day. Fatigue is piling up inside me, and I must try not to add to it.

The boat is close-hauled, and I shall have to tack towards the island if the wind remains in the north-west. But that does not matter; one hour makes no difference, especially as the boat will stay on course with the helm lashed when she is close-hauled. This frees me from the labour of steering, and allows me to get on with other jobs. Spray breaking over the bows prevents me from removing the winch cover to see what has gone wrong, but that will be my first job when we get to Jenny Lind Island.

The wind seems to me to grow colder.

'It smells to me like ice! Not that again!'

But these words are said without much conviction. The wind gets steadily colder and the waves diminish. There could be no clearer warning. Pack-ice is not far away. I can also see ice-blink to the north.

Soon afterwards I can see a thin white line on the horizon, a little to the right of Jenny Lind Island, which is now in sight.

'It was only to be expected.'

'Mind it doesn't block the way to Jenny Lind Island!'

'It can't do that, damn it!'

'Just you watch!'

At midday, with the bay already in sight, I have to turn back. The pack is solid—10/10ths multiyear polar ice. It is impossible to go on. If I did, there would probably be no way of getting out of it. A boat has no hope of getting clear when such large masses of ice are involved. The bay would not be a good place to winter in; it is too open to the sea.

It should here be noted that there is little real information about the problems of wintering in the ice, and the literature on the subject is full of traditional ideas without any real foundation.

First of all it must be understood that the freezing of a stretch of water around a boat does not of itself create any serious pressure on the hull. Most of the fishing boats in Greenland remain afloat through the winter, without any damage, in spite of their traditional construction out of wood. What is dangerous is the thrust exercised on the ice by wind or current, when the frozen surface is very extensive.

This means that it is better to winter in a small bay rather than a large one. Also, to avoid the thrust of ice coming from outside, it is necessary that the bay be shut off as far as possible by some natural obstacle—an island behind which one can take shelter, or a bar which will prevent large masses of ice from intruding. Finally, the bay must be sheltered from the prevailing winds, so that the swell caused by the storm cannot break up the ice into pieces which could drive against the hull and hole it.

It is also important not to winter in waters which are too shallow. One must beware of the water freezing right to the bottom, for in that case the thaw will be very slow, and the boat will remain imprisoned in the ice until very late in the following season.

If the crew stays on board using up stores of food and water, the total weight of the boat and its contents will gradually decrease. In this case it is important to saw away the ice at the stern of the vessel. For when the thaw begins, she will rise abruptly in the water, and the propeller must be free to rise with her.

Williwaw slowly gets clear of the pack. The characteristics of the ice are different from those forecast, which makes me think that it must have forced its way into Queen Maud Gulf from the north. The pack-ice of McClintock Channel has probably spilled over into Larsen Sound and Franklin Strait, which explains the difficulties we had in James Ross Strait. It must also have invaded Victoria Strait and so found its way through to Queen Maud Gulf. McClintock Channel seldom thaws, and its ice is therefore generally several years old. Franklin and his men perished in similar circumstances, being trapped by ice from McClintock Channel. Today, having seen the huge size of its floes, I can understand that the *Terror* and the *Erebus* had no hope of escape. As for *Williwaw* it seems logical to look for open water further to the south.

It is nearly 1800. The decision to go further south was a good one, and the pack gradually begins to look less dense. After covering about ten miles, I reach the edge of the pack and move into an area covered with scattered ice. I can now turn west again. The sun is visible, and this of course makes navigation much simpler.

I suddenly remember that the winch is out of order, and put the boat on automatic pilot for a little. But the compass is still completely wild, and the boat starts to veer in all directions. I finally have to heave to in order to dismantle the winch. Fortunately it is nothing worse than a broken belt. A new belt is soon in position, and I can go on again, knowing that all is well.

Last night I was afraid that the weather would deteriorate, but it seems to have steadied again and sailing conditions are pleasant this afternoon. Nevertheless, we must find an anchorage as soon as possible. I want to reach Melbourne Island, and hope to get there before dark. As it turns out, I catch sight of the island before sunset, but have to use radar for the actual approach.

At 2300 the anchor touches bottom. I am dead tired, but happy; progress has been very good and I have almost completed the crossing of Queen Maud Gulf. I sleep a few hours, but the prospect —accidents apart—of being able to reach Cambridge Bay in the next day's sailing gets me up early, and we are on our way by 5.

I have just had radio contact with Noël. I ask him to tell my friends on the *Bernier* about the difficulties I experienced yesterday, and to let them know that there is open water to the south of Queen Maud Gulf.

I report developments regularly to the *Bernier*. I also told them, a few days ago, that *Williwaw* touched bottom three miles off Kent Bay.

This does not mean that I do not want to keep my lead. On the contrary, I am doing and shall do all that I can to stay ahead of them. But this rivalry must be reconciled with my duties as a man and as a sailor. I give them all the information I can; but as soon as I have switched off my transmitter I devote myself entirely to getting on with the voyage, determined not to let them overtake me.

It will be difficult. There are five of them against one of me. But this is a challenge which I have set myself. There is no question about it, I want *Williwaw* to be the first sailing vessel (after the *Gjøa*) to complete the North-West Passage; and I am quite sure that on board the *Bernier* they are discussing how they can trump my ace. That's quite natural, and indeed anything else would be truly surprising.

I try to find out the present position of the *Bernier* but Noël had no definite news. He thinks they must be somewhere in Peel Sound. He will try to get some more information as soon as he can.

The western part of Queen Maud Gulf becomes progressively narrower until it passes into Dease Strait, which in turn leads on to Coronation Gulf. In the neighbourhood of Melbourne Island, the line of the coast leads off towards the north-west, which takes me back into higher latitudes. We soon run into ice again, and at 0700 I am halted by a 6/10ths to 7/10ths pack, which seems to be completely impenetrable. As before, it is formed of multiyear ice, 4 to

10 metres high. There is no proper horizon, and the eye cannot penetrate far into the chaos of the pack. I decide to turn away and observe the scene from a reasonable distance. It seems to me that I should be able to make my way forward if I hug the south coast. Obviously, I don't want to do anything silly; if it's too dangerous, it will be better to turn back to Melbourne Island and wait for better conditions. Having got back into relatively open water, I take a few minutes to check the depths shown on the chart, and am irked to note that the depths along the coast have not been surveyed, except at the entrance to Dease Strait. Nevertheless, I make my way into a clear stretch of water near the shore, entrusting myself to the dark blue colour of the water and the height of the floating ice between my boat and the shore.

In this way I succeed in making some progress, trying to work my way into the fringe of the pack, so as to increase my distance from the shore and lessen the danger of running aground.

At about 1225 I reach the MacAlpine Islands. Climbing the mast, I see a dark line ahead on the horizon. My heart beats faster; I hope this is not a mirage. There is ice round the islands, and for a moment it seems to be impassable. But I know that there is open water beyond the barrier, and that stimulates me to go on.

Finally I force my way through. Dease Strait is about ten miles away. Cambridge Bay is on the opposite side, and I cannot reach it without going back into the pack. The decision does not take me long. Never mind about anchoring, we're going on!

22

From Pearce Point to the Beaufort Sea: Saved by a Storm

'We're going on.' The decision is soon taken. One chooses the lesser of two evils, and the open water of Dease Strait is certainly more tempting than the pack-ice which blocks the route to Cambridge Bay. But the choice does nothing to lessen my backlog of sleep. I have had practically none during the last 48 hours: little or none at the anchorage by the Nordenskiold reef, and only a few hours off Melbourne Island; and now the rest I had been promising myself at Cambridge Bay has also vanished into limbo. How long will it be before there is another chance? Dease Strait does not appear to offer any protected anchorages.

The most disturbing thing of all is that the lack of sleep is not producing a normal reaction. Though fatigue has been piling up inside me for weeks, my mind has ceased to accept the idea of rest. I feel stimulated to an extraordinary extent. As soon as I lie down, I want to be off again, to go on, to advance towards my goal. I am like a sledge-dog who will go on pulling till he drops dead, unless his master unharnesses him. And I realise that I cannot unharness myself. Being back on my own has over-motivated me. If I cannot calm myself down, I shall collapse in my tracks like a husky with a bad master.

What am I to do to lower the pressure? What I need, come to think of it, is a diversion. An absorbing physical occupation would probably do the trick. But what can I do? I cannot leave the helm. If I were to heave to in the hope of finding relief, I should feel so guilty about not making any progress towards my goal that my agitation would make rest totally impossible.

To identify a problem and try to solve it is an important step towards finding the answer. I promise myself that I will be sensible enough to avoid pushing myself beyond measure. Meanwhile, I try to put ice, sleep, stress and worry out of my mind and devote myself —calmly and without any hurried movements—to verifying the state of the compass, at the same time continuing to navigate the boat.

And, after all, why not listen to some Beethoven? The Fifth Piano Concerto, for example, which has so many happy memories attached to it . . . the quiet beauty of the beginning of the second movement can only calm me down. I have always claimed that I am never really alone, and now I am taking Beethoven as my companion.

The swaying motion imparted to the boat by the light swell which marks the waters of the strait seem to correspond closely to the rhythm of the music, and gradually I feel myself melting into it. I am not listening to the concerto now—I am part of it. It is not Beethoven who is freeing his heart from all that oppresses it, but myself. When I reach the end of the work, the final staccato, I have reached the end of all my worries, at least for a time. Then the Pastoral Symphony pours peace into my soul. Thank you, dear master!

On the evening of August 29, having covered the 65 miles of Dease Strait at a good speed, we enter Coronation Gulf. *Williwaw* has done marvels; for my part I have again been busy trying to check the reliability of the compass.

We have not encountered any ice at all, and I have been sailing under genuinely relaxed conditions for the first time for many days. The compass has gained stability, and I have been able to use the automatic pilot. The heeling error is difficult to evaluate, but I have noticed that the boat pays off when she heels, a tendency which will take us away from the Victoria Island coast which we have been hugging, if the wind remains in the north. It is 10 o'clock. Darkness has fallen, but I have kept under way in the absence of any good places to anchor. It must be added that the moon is full and visibility is quite adequate. The wind has freshened, and the boat is heeling more heavily, increasing the instability of the compass so that I am concerned about our route. A lunar azimuth enables me to check our heading in a general way, but the wind is gusting and the steering of the boat is correspondingly erratic.

I steer manually for a time. Crouched in the cockpit, I try to avoid the biting cold. Then the wind gradually veers to the east, so that it is blowing from astern. The heel is reduced, and I can switch to the automatic pilot again. My hands are blue and my fingers hurt.

The hours pass slowly by, and in the morning, after another sleepless night, I feel extremely tired. The wind has steadied, and is blowing from the east, force 8 to 9. I handed the mainsail during the night, and only the storm-jib is still up. The shore is no longer visible, and we must be somewhat to the south of the ideal route. Finally I decide to seek shelter behind Edinburgh Island, and set a course for the coast. But there is still a long way to go, and I shall not be able to rest just yet.

Towards 1700, in pelting rain and visibility to match, I finally identify the gloomy outline of Edinburgh Island, and at 1800 we are anchored in the shelter of its north-west corner. The anchor gets a good hold, and does not drag in spite of the gusts. Visibility is down to under a mile. It is raining cats and dogs. I go straight to bed and fall asleep almost immediately.

The storm demanded the physical exertion which I need to give. I was soaked by spray and rain; I felt the familiar slap of salt water across my face. There is always a silver lining; and the bad weather also provided the mental diversion which I needed. I wake before dawn, after nine hours of good sleep, and bake some bread. In the meantime, I cook myself a substantial meal. The wind has dropped and the moon is shining again in a relatively clear sky. I am inwardly at peace. The mileage covered has again been exceptionally good; with the help of Providence, this season is developing better than I had hoped.

Yesterday I put the following note in the log-book, at the foot of the page: '*About 1000 miles to go to Point Barrow!*'

This was the first time I had specifically recorded my current position in relation to the completion of the North-West Passage. I am gradually beginning to believe in the possibility of getting through without spending more than one arctic winter. This makes me very happy. I shall be back with my family that much sooner; and also both the risks to be run and the financial expense will be appreciably reduced. It would be splendid if I could reach Herschel Island before the winter. But that means covering a further 600 miles or more.

The distance could be regarded as trifling or enormous, according to the circumstances. 600 miles of open water is only a few days' sailing; but in pack-ice the same distance could take years to cover. When Amundsen left Gjøa Haven after the winter of 1904, he was not able to reach Herschel Island in a complete season's sailing. At the moment I have no certain information about the state of the ice in the western Arctic. Besides, we are gently approaching the end of the season—at the end of the last century, the whalers operating in the Beaufort Sea arranged their programme so that they would round Point Barrow on their return journey before September 1. It was not considered impossible to leave the Arctic a few days later, but it was always dangerous, and more than one ship was lost through missing the usual date. Even before September 1 there is no guarantee that it will be possible to pass this, the most northerly point of the United States, and it has happened more than once that Point Barrow has remained impassable for the whole season.

In 1871, for example, the entire American whaling fleet, comprising dozens of ships, was caught to the east of Point Barrow. The crews were saved, but all the ships, without exception, were lost. The survival of the walruses of the Beaufort Sea—and that of the Eskimos who lived on them—is probably due to the loss of these whaling vessels, a loss which was fortunately never completely made good.

How far can I go before the pack becomes completely solid again? Who knows? From now on, I must look at every anchorage with the critical eye of a man searching for winter shelter.

Shortly before 6 in the morning we are again under way. The weather is good: clear sky, light wind from west-north-west (force 3), sea calm, visibility good.

We pass the Duke of York Islands. The English name of this group reminds me that Franklin's first expedition passed this way. Between 1819 and 1822, that expedition explored Coronation Gulf, so called in honour of the accession of George IV.

Lady Franklin Point, which marks the entrance to Dolphin and Union Strait, also owes its name to the same expedition.

The morning starts off very pleasantly, but about 1000, as I approach the entrance to Dolphin and Union Strait, which connects Coronation Gulf and Amundsen Gulf, the sky clouds over from the west, and a strong wind gets up from the north at very short notice.

For a moment I think of sheltering in Austin Bay, behind Lady Franklin Point, but it is several miles astern, and I do not want to lengthen my route. So I sail on, looking out for other possibilities.

When I reach Cache Point, which is already well into the strait, I sight a ship at anchor. This is the *Baffin*, from Ottawa, an oceanographic research ship with which I have sometimes talked over the radio.

A lot of people come on deck to greet me as I go by. In addition to the crew, there are a good many scientists on the *Baffin*. Many arms wave, good wishes are exchanged by megaphone, and there is some cheering. One man even throws his cap in the air as a sign of welcome. The wind, naturally enough, carries it away; I can see from the poor fellow's sheepish expression that he was not expecting that to happen. I conclude that he must be a scientist—a sailor would never be so absent-minded!

The wind is really very strong and progress is slow, so I decide to avoid unnecessary fatigue and anchor in the lee of Cache Point.

As soon as the anchor chain is taut, I notice that the point is washed by a current of three or four knots.

I hope it won't be too difficult to weigh anchor! As it is still relatively early, I cook myself a good meal and get on with some maintenance jobs until it is time for my radio contact with Belgium. The wind is blowing furiously outside, but the bottom appears to be firm and the boat seems to be perfectly safe.

I have just learnt from Noël that the *Bernier* is at 60° 34' N., 99° 00' W., in Simpson Strait.

So I'm five days ahead! It's not much—the least mishap could change everything, and the *Bernier*, with a crew of five, can easily travel day and night in ice-free waters.

If I were in Réal Bouvier's shoes, I would not, however, bet too heavily on this possibility. Even admitting that *Williwaw* has to stop for an average of 8 out of 24 hours every day, the *Bernier* would still take 15 days to catch up, sailing day and night, and other things being equal. But in fact other things are *not* equal. *Williwaw* is faster than the *Bernier* and much better prepared for independent navigation. So I'm not really afraid of being overtaken, though a mishap is still possible which could change the picture completely.

I cannot help thinking again about the relativity of our motives. I left Europe a year later than the *Bernier* left Canada; I have consequently already made up a deficit of more than twelve months.

Yet the couple of hours, or even minutes, which may finally separate us at Bering Strait, where the North-West Passage ends, are of far greater weight. That is a pity, but I can do nothing about it. Only one runner can come in first.

Visibility was much reduced during the high winds yesterday and last night, but it improves this morning, and I am able to weigh anchor and get under way at about 8. The north-east wind is still strong, at force 5 to 6, and it would be pleasanter to stay a little longer in the shelter of Cache Point; but I must keep going and take advantage of the favourable wind.

I was afraid that it would be difficult to get the anchor up, for the current was drifting the boat across the line of the chain. But this morning the current has vanished, and the chain is leading dead ahead, making everything easier than expected.

The wind drops during the day, and towards the end of the afternoon, at 1700 we pass Cape Besley, keeping clear of the reef which fringes it. The weather is good and sailing conditions are pleasant, with the sails filling well, and I have seen no ice all day; so I decide to sail on during the night. The compass is steadier now, but the heeling error persists, which is difficult to evaluate because the angle of heel is not constant. This morning, however, I had Liston Island on the horizon and was able to make some observations and improve the accuracy of the compass.

The night passes without noteworthy incidents. At about 0200, we round Clifton Point and enter Amundsen Gulf. It is fairly difficult to identify the details of the coast by the radar. The shore is low-lying, and only the delta of the Croker River shows up well on the screen. The first squall of a new storm hits us just as we arrive opposite the delta, fifteen miles beyond Clifton Point, blowing right on the nose. I am compelled to go on to the other tack, away from the coast. The wind gradually strengthens, and the sea runs higher. Progress is slow, and it is very cold.

Dawn finds *Williwaw* tossing in a short, choppy, unpleasant sea. I am tired; this further sleepless night weighs me down, and I look out apprehensively at the green, marbled surface of Amundsen Gulf, across which long trains of spume are chased by the wind.

I tack several times, wanting to press on at any cost. There is no shelter on this coast. From Bernard Harbour in Dolphin and Union Strait to Pearce Point Harbour, 80 miles further to the west-north-west, there is no reasonably safe bay; and we must not get blocked between the two harbours.

So I try to go on in spite of everything; but at about 1000 on September 1 no further progress is possible, and I have to heave-to.

I must get some sleep. Unfortunately the slow leak previously detected in the master cylinder of the hydraulic steering control has the effect that the rudder, instead of remaining locked to one side, slowly creeps back to a central position, allowing the boat to get under way. I have to attend to this at regular intervals, and the alarm clock periodically gets me out of my bunk.

Coming on deck shortly after 2200, I notice that it has begun to rain. The wind has lessened, and seems to be settling down to a steady force 6. I take advantage of this to get under way; but can make practically no headway close-hauled. Finally I decide to let the boat run before the wind and get away from the coast so as to have more room for manoeuvre.

At about 2330 a violent squall compels me to heave-to again. The wind has veered more towards the north, and I am not sorry to have gained more sea-room.

The night never seems to end. I am afraid of sleeping through the alarm. I doze a little in the cockpit, but I am not happy about this, and decide to try and keep myself busy. I call up *Baffin* to report my position, but they evidently do not hear me, and *Pandora II* answers instead. During the conversation which follows, I learn that *Pandora II* is an oceanographic research ship which has been commissioned to do some survey work near Banks Island, a good hundred miles to the north-west of our present position.

The conversation is a very friendly one, and Harry the third officer and Bob the radio operator give me all the encouragement they can, which does something to offset the disappointment I feel when they tell me that there is a gale warning for the next 24 hours. The *Pandora II* will report my position to the Canadian Coastguard. Harry suggests that we should speak again tomorrow, so that he can bring me up to date with the latest weather forecasts.

Their friendly kindness was a great comfort; and their final good wishes for a successful voyage have given me fresh energy.

'Come on Willy! What are you grumbling about? Grit your

teeth! You'll soon have to stop for the winter, and then you'll be able to sleep as much as you like!'

At about 0700 the wind drops to force 6. The seas are still high, and I decide to wait a little longer before getting under way. Luckily I have been able to sleep a few hours, but I am still worried about my physical condition. I am afraid of exceeding my strength, and, if I still have some reserves, I would like to save them for the final spurt.

At 0800, realising that I must go on as soon as possible, I get under way under jib and mizzen. There is a fresh wind from the north-north-east, and the sea is choppy and uncomfortable. The sky gradually clears, and a pallid sun lights up the damp and chilly morning scene from time to time.

I do not know exactly where we are. We have undoubtedly lost ground—but how much? The low-lying, misty coast has no clearly recognisable features, and I must look elsewhere to determine my position. The depth of the water is a better indication, and the echo-sounder suggests that we have drifted a considerable distance and are now back inside Dolphin and Union Strait, more than 30 miles short of the position we had reached when we hove-to.

For a time I hope I am wrong about this; but at midday the Croker River delta shows up on the radar screen again, and I have to accept the evidence—while we were hove-to, we lost at least 30 miles of distance and 24 hours of useful time.

On September 3, shortly after midnight, just when I have made up the distance so unhappily lost, the wind backs to the west and suddenly strengthens. I am afraid that I may have to heave-to again, but I cannot make up my mind to do so. That would mean losing valuable time all over again, and running the risk of being caught by the pack. The *Pandora II* had reported that she was in ice 150 miles from our present position, and, in this weather, it would not take long for the pack to come down on us.

No, we must stay under way whatever happens; we must claw to windward again. The fighting spirit is needed once more. I crowd sail, sheeting in as hard as possible. I cannot face another sleepless night without the stimulus of a struggle which will help me to endure the consequent fatigue; I must have that stimulus if I am to be able to tap the very last of my resources. I am more convinced than ever that it is best to programme one's efforts so as to avoid

excessive fatigue; but in the present case I have no choice. I must
see this through. I am still capable of a final spurt, but a longer
period of concentration would finish me. I must not delude myself:
if I do not quickly reach the shelter of Pearce Point, the whole
enterprise will probably come to an end somewhere along the
intervening 65 miles. The wind keeps strengthening. The sails,
stretched taut, strain at the masts, which groan and heel beneath
their pressure.

The agony of my boat enters into my being like the agony of a
friend. My jaws close with a powerful contraction, which hurts
right up to my ears. The will to fight is born in the battle itself, and
the intimate link which unites me with my boat and with all that
she represents or evokes is a basic stimulant. We shall never surrender! Turning my face away for a moment from the lashing
spray, I look astern, and see my ensign torn to ribbons by the wind.
No matter—'*Je maintiendrai*' none the less!

It was a terrible night, but my trusty *Williwaw* won through, and
we reached Pearce Point this morning. I let go the anchor. Dazed,
with bloodshot eyes and aching face, I watch the chain run out. My
hand is stiffened by the cold so that I cannot grasp the pulpit, and
have to hold on to the life-line with the crook of my elbow to prevent myself falling. It has been a time of great physical pain.

During the night the wind rose to force 9. A continual stream of
spindrift rose from the stem, and was whisked away by the icy
wind. I was chilled to the bone in my wet clothes. My eyes,
scanning the darkness for any sign of an oncoming ice-pack have
suffered the harsh impact of the damp sou'wester and the sting of
the salt.

A few miles from Pearce Point, I had to hand the mizzen. The
mast was bending right over and was going to break at any moment.
The engine was going flat out, but we were making hardly any
headway. What a nightmare! I tried to warm my frozen hands
between my thighs, but to no effect. The pain in my fingers made
me groan aloud. . . . But now the anchor-chain has run right out. I
am still in the bows, bent double, almost on my knees, with my
arms crooked around the guard-rail. 'For God's sake, Willy! Stand
up and go below into the warm!'

I am extremely tired. It is 0830 on September 3 1977.

Before I can turn in I must investigate a leakage of oil from the engine which I have noticed. On closer inspection, I discover another broken bolt on the forward engine-bracket. Fortunately I manage to extract the embedded end of the bolt, and replacement should be a simple matter. A long search, however, fails to discover a spare bolt with the same thread. Finally I have to take a Whitworth bolt out of the engine-casing to replace the one that has broken. Then I clean up: a ventilation duct has let in some rainwater, and I take a bath in a bucket to get rid of the thick layer of salt which is clinging to my skin; then I cook a meal and turn in. I thank Providence for His help, and go to sleep, rocked by the choppy sea raised by the gale.

On the morning of September 4, after a long and good sleep, things take on a rosier hue. The wind has dropped, and a timid ray of sunshine lights up the rocky landscape of Pearce Point, which has sheltered me so well. All things considered, it's fantastic to be here. My morale tends towards euphoria!

I keep my radio appointment with the *Pandora II*, and Harry, helpful as ever, tells me that two technicians are camped at Pearce Point, looking after a Decca transmitter; they are in possession of the most recent weather forecasts.

Harry says that the weather is unsettled, and he advises me not to leave the anchorage until I have full information about the way it is developing. He also tells me that the Mackenzie Delta is at present free from ice, and that the pack which covers the Beaufort Sea has moved back to a distance of about 15 miles off Cape Bathurst.

Cape Bathurst is an important milestone on our route, being the most northerly point of continental Canada except for Boothia Peninsula, and also marking the entrance to the Beaufort Sea. The cape has a bad reputation, and is said to be often difficult to pass. This opportunity to round the cape fills me with delight, and I should like to go straight on without any delay. As for the weather forecasts, I shall have to manage without them.

On second thoughts, however, I do not like to ignore Harry's advice. That would be to show little respect for his undoubted common sense; and if tomorrow he asks for news of the two technicians, what shall I be able to tell him?

'Come on, Willy! Lower the dinghy!'

Having spotted a camp on the southern shore of the bay, with two large canvas tents, one khaki and the other red, I row over to it without delay. As I approach the shore, I notice a man waiting for me on the shingle. I can see at once that we are going to be friends.

'Nice to see you. Welcome.' Simple, sincere words of greeting, accompanied by a pleasant smile.

We walk straight over to one of the tents, where the other technician is waiting for us. 'Coffee, eggs and bacon—what d'you say?'

'Yes, please!'

'O.K., take a seat.'

The tent serves as workshop, kitchen, living-room and bedroom. It is fairly cluttered, and I have to use my elbows to make room for my place at the table among the electronic accessories and wires.

The younger of the two, whose name is Bruce, has apparently managed to find the gas stove under a heap of saucepans, and the smell of bacon is already mingling with the smell of insulating varnish given off by the electrical equipment. We're soon deep in conversation, all asking questions at once.

I learn that the season is nearly over for my two friends and that a helicopter is going to come and pick them up in two days time. They have to take everything with them down to the last bolt, including their dustbin. They have very definite instructions: nothing must be left on site, no rubbish, no trace that they have been here.

It has not always been like that. When the D.E.W.Line (Distant Early Warning Line) was operational, there was an important station at Pearce Point. All the buildings and equipment are still there. The personnel left one fine morning, leaving everything behind. Large fuel tanks stand at the entrance to the bay, and the powerful electric generator is intact. If I had to winter here, I should like to start it up again, to spare my batteries.

Time passes quickly when people have a lot to say to each other, and a good deal of the morning is gone when, after a final embrace, I get back into the dinghy.

Rowing is a problem, for the bottom of the dinghy is full of provisions which Bruce and his colleague have pressed on me.

'That much less for the "chopper" to carry!' they tell me.

'Thank you, my friends; I'm not really short of food, but I've stuffed myself so thoroughly with Belgian *cassoulet grand-mère* that it's coming out of my ears. Your "chuck-waggon stew" will make a delicious change. As for the fresh oranges and grapefruit, I haven't had anything like that for months . . . But above all the warmth of your welcome has restored my morale. Thank you for everything.'

Back on the *Williwaw*, I realise that I have completely forgotten to ask about the weather forecasts. Never mind! My visit to their camp has been so rewarding that I'm almost ashamed of my original hesitation. I was afraid it would all be tiresome—but in fact I have come back feeling better and quite relaxed. If Harry or his colleagues talk to me about the two technicians at Pearce Point, I shall not be in the least embarrassed; on the contrary I shall be able to compliment them on their excellent advice.

This has been yet another lesson again that will-power is all important, and that listlessness is more damaging than physical exertion. My morale is at its highest point as I leave the harbour for the open sea. There is not much wind, and visibility is generally good. Cape Parry is rounded without difficulty, and Cape Bathurst lies 80 miles ahead. I plan to sail on through the night, and hope to reach Cape Bathurst during the morning of tomorrow, September 5. That would be another splendid advance.

Remembering the state of exhaustion in which I arrived at Pearce Point, I resolve to be very careful indeed. I endeavour to eat as well as possible (greatly helped by the fact that I now have something new to try), to rest as much as possible, and to avoid irritation by keeping everything around me in perfect order.

My navigation reflects my mental qualities; and I deliberately try to keep it as precise as possible, as a continuous, reassuring reminder to myself of what those qualities are.

I am aware of my fatigue, but not dominated by it. I am inwardly relaxed and at rest, and I feel as if I were watching myself from outside. Though I am directly concerned by what happens to me, I keep a certain distance between myself and events; and this is the tremendous advantage of inward tranquility.

Extracts from my log-book for September 5 1977:
'It is barely dawn. Cape Bathurst is not far away now, and I have not met with any ice! I thought I saw ice-blink once or twice during the night, but each time it turned out to be the light of the moon filtering through a strip of clear sky.

'1548 G.M.T. (0748 local time): we are doubling Observation Point. This takes us into Beaufort Sea. Cape Bathurst itself does not measure up to the immensity of my gratitude to Providence for allowing me to come this far.

'I think I feel lonelier than ever before at this moment, when the North-West Passage seems to be really within my grasp. At this moment of great happiness, I should have liked to have a friend on board, with whom I could have exchanged an embrace to celebrate the triumph of a team and the union of two men in a common will to win through; and to mark a success which each partner achieves as much for his companion as for himself—an embrace the memory of which will make an imperishable link between two human souls.'

I close the log-book and look out to sea. I notice that the water of the Beaufort Sea is green—not the deep green of a Polynesian lagoon, but a pale, bright green, bright as the new hope in my heart —the hope of reaching Herschel Island before winter.

23

Water in the Fuel!

The Beaufort Sea lies along the northern coast of Canada and Alaska to the west of Cape Bathurst. It is part of the Arctic Ocean, and is consequently subject to the influence of the entire polar ice-pack. Although the wider movements of the ice are controlled almost entirely by the thrust of the prevailing winds, it remains possible, and even probable, that those movements will be totally at variance with the meteorological conditions observed locally. It is therefore wise to consider weather forecasts based on these local observations as extremely speculative.

This means that, since I have no information covering conditions in the Beaufort Sea as a whole, I can form no idea of what tomorrow will bring. My hope of reaching Herschel Island is therefore no more than a hope. I may find the way barred before I get there, so that I have to look for shelter on the way. It might be in Liverpool Bay, for example, somewhere along Tuktoyaktuk Peninsula, in Kugmalik Bay, or behind one of the many islands in the Mackenzie Delta.

In 1905, Amundsen left Gjøa Haven on August 13. At the end of the same month, he was blocked near King Point in Mackenzie Bay, where he had to winter, 30 miles short of Herschel Island. The continental shelf stretches up to 70 miles out from the coast and is shallow, so that the danger of running aground is added to the other navigational difficulties. Off Tuktoyaktuk Peninsula lie a large number of small, low-lying, dome-shaped islands known as the 'Pingos'; fog is frequent in this area; and the currents caused by the outflow of the waters of the Mackenzie River make dead reckoning very unreliable; so there is no margin for mistakes, and navigation can become a very complicated matter.

It cannot be long now before I go into winter quarters, and I have used the engine several times since leaving Gjøa Haven. I should therefore be glad of a chance to fill up my fuel tank. I mentioned this to Harry (of the *Pandora*) this morning, and he told me that I could probably find some fuel at Tuktoyaktuk. But this would involve a detour which I would rather not make. The harbour of Tuk is off my route, and I would rather go on to Herschel Island, if possible. I also mentioned that my charts cover only the Canadian Arctic, and that I have no charts for the coasts of Alaska.

This is not the result of negligence on my part. My plan was to ensure that the charts I bought would be up-to-date at the moment when I needed to use them; but I assumed that that moment was still several years away, because I never hoped to get as far as this in so short a time. In any case, the leg from here to Herschel Island poses no problems, because I have all the necessary charts with me.

Several hams have told me that the Canadian public is passionately interested in my voyage, and that certain papers are publishing news about me on the front page. I wonder what they can be finding to say, for I have not seen a journalist since I met Kununguak Fleischer at Egedesminde, and I very much doubt whether his prose has been reproduced in Canada. It seems more likely that the Coastguard, to whom I report my daily position, has been putting out a communiqué. Or could it be Harry, in Vancouver? We talk almost every day and Harry, too, has been following my progress closely. Be that as it may, it is pleasant to know that other people are participating in the ups and downs of my expedition. The knowledge that I have already established a significant record, by getting so far in such a short time, adds to my pleasure.

The *Pandora II*, my guardian angel, has also been in touch to give me the position of two offshore oil rigs, which I immediately marked on the chart.

September 5 is a pleasant day, and we make good progress; but towards evening the wind gets up. (The barometer has been falling since September 3.) I am tired; I have had practically no sleep since we left Pearce Point which means that I have again been on my feet for nearly 36 hours. If the wind continues to strengthen, I shall have to anchor for the night, for there can be no question of going on blindly in the dark in these shallow waters.

Visibility is reduced, and the approach to the coast, which rises very little above sea-level, requires considerable care. Fortunately I sight land a little before nightfall, and finally anchor in the shelter of Atkinson Point, on the Tuk Peninsula, at about 2100.

Wind from the south-east, force 6–7, sea calm, in the lee of the shore. We have covered 75 miles since leaving Cape Bathurst. Tuk harbour is 40 miles off, and its entrance must certainly be free from ice. Herschel Island is 160 miles ahead. My plan is to reach this historic anchorage, where so many whaling ships spent the winter during the last century. If I run into trouble, I can make for Tuk, where conditions for wintering are equally good. Everything will be decided in the next few days, and I shall soon know the answer.

After a windy night, I am up as soon as there is light in the sky. The days are getting gradually shorter. Today, September 6, the sun rises at 0436 over Tuk Peninsula and sets at 2228. So it is light when at 0545 I weigh anchor and set off.

After making sail, I feel the need to pass water, and am conscious of an uncomfortable sensation which starts in my kidneys and works its way further down. I hope that a kidney stone is not about to start on its travels! That would be a catastrophe at the present moment . . . To tell the truth, I know very well what the form is. I have had this trouble several times before and know the symptoms well. The discomfort I have just experienced clearly indicates that a stone has broken adrift, and is now travelling freely in my renal pelvis.

This is naturally worrying. I knew, from an X-ray taken before I left Belgium, that my right kidney contained two small stones. One of them must have detached itself, and in the normal course of things it will soon pass into the urethra. I have therefore little chance of escaping a painful attack in the near future. Let's hope that it does not happen before we reach shelter!

There is excellent news, on the other hand, when I speak to the *Pandora*. The third officer has been in touch with the *Nahidik*, a Canadian ship which is carrying out geological research in the Mackenzie Delta, and has arranged for her to provide me with fuel. The *Nahidik* is not far away, and a rendezvous has been arranged near Pullen Island. I am asked to get directly in touch with her at a suitable time so that we can co-ordinate our movements. The crew of the *Pandora* are really wonderful, and Harry, with his captain's blessing, is doing everything he can to help me. Every message ends with words of encouragement and best wishes for success. I think they will be as disappointed as I myself if I have a mishap.

All this keeps my morale high, in spite of the sombre prospect for the next few days arising from the kidney trouble. Anyway, I am trying not to think too much about it. I must go on as if nothing had happened until the crisis comes.

I have been in contact with the *Nahidik*. She is at present at 69° 42' N., 133° 28' W., in the middle of Kugmalik Bay, to the west of Tuk. This places her at about 40 miles from Atkinson Point, which we left this morning.

The wind has dropped a little, and the weather is relatively fine this afternoon. Conditions are good for two vessels to tie up alongside. Luck seems to be on my side; but when I reach the agreed meeting-place, I can see no sign of the *Nahidik*. Am I really at the agreed place? The *Nahidik* had mentioned that an old cargo ship was anchored near at hand, and I can in fact see this vessel to port. Is the *Nahidik* perhaps lying out of sight behind her? I sail towards the cargo vessel, and discover, as I get closer, that she is the *Canmar Explorer*. But the *Nahidik* is definitely not here.

I call up the *Canmar Explorer* on the radio, and learn that the *Nahidik* has already sailed for Pullen Island, where she will wait for me. The captain of the *Canmar Explorer* has heard that I have no charts for the journey to Barrow Point, and asks me if I would like to come alongside so that he can throw the necessary chart down to me. 'You never know,' he says. 'You might need it.' I take his advice, and come close enough for them to toss down a weighted plastic bag containing the U.S. chart *Herschel Island—Point Barrow*, accompanied by friendly wishes for a successful voyage and several tins of sardines!

Then, after a final '*Bon voyage!*', I set course for Pullen Island which is about 15 miles further west. I arrive at sunset, and find the *Nahidik* ready to supply me with fuel.

They give me a royal reception. The captain, surrounded by members of the scientific staff, bids me welcome, and it is the chief engineer in person who passes me the fuelling hose.

I note that this is a length of rubber tubing. This disturbs me for a moment, because rubber is soluble in Diesel; but as the arrangements are all ready, I say nothing, thinking that no harm will be done if the operation is carried out quickly enough.

Then they invite me on board. The captain lends me his cabin so that I can take a shower—which, incidentally, I need very badly. Then I have supper and a pleasant evening with the crew. It is midnight when I return to *Williwaw*, loaded with a large case of provisions. As I move off and anchor for the night, the *Nahidik* is getting under way to pursue her geological researches. As I lie in my bunk, at peace with the world, well fed and enjoying the feeling of clean sheets against a clean skin, I think gratefully about everybody who has helped me, including those who have given me no more than an approving look or an encouraging word.

It is the fellow-feeling, the warmth and the brotherhood that are important, no matter how they are expressed.

And here we see the difference between self-sufficiency and independence. I like to run my life in accordance with my personal logic, but I have neither the intention nor the wish to free myself from the dependence that may result from a friendship, an ideal or a freely given promise. And this distinction makes me reflect that, though I love solitude, I would not want to be alone in life. I do not want to renounce the world of my fellow men, but to avoid the arbitrary features of the way it is organised.

Herschel Island is 100 miles away. I feel that it is within my grasp, and first light finds us already under way. According to the most recent weather reports received by the *Nahidik*, a strong south-westerly is forecast for the next 24 hours. But it is still calm this morning, and I am in a hurry to get on.

Navigation in these waters is a ticklish matter. We have to cross the delta of the Mackenzie River, and the *Sailing Directions* indicate that the outflow of its waters causes a three-knot current which sets towards the north.

Fortunately I am able to get an idea of my position from the soundings; in the absence of adequate visibility, I accordingly steer by the sea bottom. The compass is still unstable, and the heeling error is difficult to evaluate.

During the afternoon, the sky gradually becomes overcast. The forecast high winds have not yet made their appearance, but the breeze which was blowing from the south-east this morning has gradually veered south-west, and then north-north-west. At present it is blowing force 4. The barometer has steadied at 1003 millibars and has stopped falling.

I have just altered course, and am aiming directly towards Thetis Bay, near Herschel Island. I have deliberately kept well out to the north; now that I have the necessary chart on board, I intend to continue to Demarcation Bay, if the wind makes up its mind to blow from the south-west, as forecast. (Demarcation Bay is on the frontier between Canada and Alaska.) In this case I shall get the benefit of an offshore wind which should, for a time at least, push back the pack-ice from the coast. If, on the other hand, the wind veers to the north-west—which would be unfavourable as far as the ice is concerned—I shall go back to my former plan and can shelter in Thetis Bay as previously intended. I have thus provided myself with two possible plans. I shall be able to keep under sail whichever wind blows.

Towards evening, the wind backs west again, and strengthens rapidly; which means that we cannot aim directly at Demarcation Bay at present. At 2050, the wind is still rising, turning to a gale as darkness falls.

The anchorage is still 7 miles away, behind the dense curtain of mist which hides the coast. Radar and echo-sounder are the basis of my navigation, and the landfall that I achieve is a model of its kind. I checked each underwater contour as I crossed it, and, despite nil visibility and rough conditions, the boat sails into the bay in perfect safety and anchors without difficulty. It is 2139 on September 7.

While cooking my supper, I check that the anchor is holding; I eat my meal and tidy up, and when bedtime comes I know that I can go to sleep in full peace of mind. Full peace of mind as far as the anchorage is concerned, that is to say; for my friends on the *Pandora II* proved to be a disturbing influence in another connection, when I signalled my position to them just now.

The dialogue took an unexpected turn:

'Willy, have you reached Herschel Island?'

'Yes, an hour ago.'

'Take a good look at the island, just above water-level; you should be able to see a light.'

'What on earth . . .!'

'Go on, stick your head out and have a look! Can you see the light?'

'Yes, I can see it.'

'Good! That's Bob Mackenzie's house. He's an Eskimo trapper who has a very nice wife. He's been away from home for nearly three months! You've been alone for a long time too . . . Get into your dinghy and go and spend the evening with little Mrs. Mackenzie! That'll give you something else to think about!'

'Listen, I'm not here for a lark. Just report my position to Frobisher Bay and get out of my hair!'

'O.K., Willy. Good night!'

They're pulling my leg, of course . . . Still, the light is really there, and the captain of the *Nahidik* also mentioned that there was someone living on Herschel Island. And after all, there's no reason to assume that such a visit must necessarily have some scabrous motive. I could very well go across, just for a little chat. No harm in that!

If I did have serious thoughts of lowering the dinghy, they did not last for long. When I went on deck and felt the impact of the wind, I soon realised that it would be lunacy to try and go ashore in weather like that. But I can't help feeling some regret as, rocked by the swell and with only the howl of the gale to keep me company, I slip into my chilly sleeping-bag.

I smile at my bad luck, and amuse myself by throwing a little oil on the flames, visualising a delightful little Eskimo girl, with winning ways . . . She works her way into my dreams as I fall asleep, and soon her igloo is transformed into an Arabian Nights palace, I see her on a Persian carpet . . . 'Oh! Lady Mackenzie . . .!'

It is still dark when I wake up. The wind has dropped a little, but it is still quite strong, and I am not sure what to do.

Herschel Island is less than 400 miles from Point Barrow, which is the last serious difficulty to be overcome. If I could reach it before the onset of winter, it would be really wonderful. But there are dangers: the *Pandora* has already left Banks Island for Point Barrow, and the *Camsel*, which is an icebreaker, is also already on her way out of the Arctic for the winter.

The *Nahidik* and the vessels sighted in the Mackenzie Delta are on their way up the river to the Great Lakes for the winter. The season is over for everybody; and I shall certainly be the last to round Point Barrow—if I can make it! And that poses another problem. There are very few places suitable for wintering on this stretch of coast, which is also directly exposed to the polar ice and to the currents which make it so dangerous. On the other hand, 400 miles could be only a few days sailing, and that is devilish tempting. Wintering on Herschel Island also has its dangers. Wherever you are in the Arctic you cannot avoid danger, and the best policy is to weigh the various risks against each other before taking a final decision.

As far as I am concerned, my health is good, my morale is very high. There is still the question of my kidney stone and its possible movements. Although I am aware of its presence, it has not caused any crisis so far. That crisis cannot be far away, but it is by no means certain that it will come in the very near future. Anyway, I have the necessary medicines, antispasmodic and sedative; but I am not altogether happy about using them, in view of my state of very great fatigue. It would be a serious matter if there were a complication which put me out of action.

Finally, the spirit of duty wins the day over the spirit of shilly-shally. If I mean to go, I must go on at once.

'And what about milady?'

'Regret her if you must, but don't look back. We're going on!'

At 0640 the anchor comes up, bringing with it some of the soil of Thetis Bay. As I put about, I can see the Mackenzies' house, standing next to the deserted camp of the Royal Canadian Mounted Police. A thin wisp of smoke rises from the chimney. It must be very pleasant in there . . .

There is still a force 5 wind when we leave Thetis Bay, but it gradually drops, and the sea, which was rough to begin with, also becomes calmer. A little later, the sun comes up, and the weather becomes really fine.

VEØMEC (the *Pandora*) informs me that the wind will shift to the south-west, which would be a great help. It is a beautiful day, and the sun has some warmth in it. The temperature is 37°F.

Towards 1600 we cross the frontier between Canada and the United States. I try to call up the United States Coastguard to notify them that we have entered their waters, but without success.

Taking advantage of the excellent weather and knowing that I must press on hard to reach Point Barrow as soon as possible, I stay under way as long as I can. But at 2245 I approach Barter Island, where there is often a good deal of ice, and I dare not go on any further in the dark. I anchor off Tapkaurak Spit, in 13 fathoms. We have covered nearly 90 miles since leaving Herschel Island— about a quarter of the distance to Point Barrow. This is an encouraging result—the more miles we cover the sooner we shall come up against any obstacles that there may be.

I know very well that final success cannot be regarded as certain before the very end of the passage. As I am not equipped to break my way through polar ice, a small stretch of solid pack would be enough to defeat me. The sooner this happens (if it must), the better will be my chances of turning back and finding shelter, and the greater my prospects of survival.

While I am getting into position to anchor, the engine stops abruptly; the stove has also gone out earlier in the evening.

I check the fuel, and am horrified to discover that the *Nahidik* has filled my tank with water. I am completely at a loss for a moment, cursing myself for not having checked the refuelling more carefully. Then I start to think logically again. The tank was not empty before we filled it up. It is unlikely that what I received from the *Nahidik* was all water, for I remember having checked the liquid at one point. But even if it were all water, my previous stock of Diesel is still in the tank. All I have to do is to pump out the water, which, because of its higher specific gravity, will be lying underneath the oil in the bottom of the tank. I proceed to test this possibility, and luckily, after I have drawn off two buckets of water, the fuel pump begins to deliver Diesel again. Probably the *Nahidik* refuelled me from the draining-tap at the bottom of her tank, and pumped out some of the condensation water which it contained. And they say you shouldn't look a gift horse in the mouth . . .!

Reassured, I clean the filters and clear the fuel lines. Warm again at last, for the stove is now working normally, I go to sleep, exhausted. But the mishap has caused the usual defensive reaction. Overmotivated, I get up shortly before dawn, and am under way again at 0354. Towards midday the fog comes down, and shortly afterwards *Williwaw* makes her way into the pack.

There is an obvious relationship between the thickness of the ice and the size of the floes. The floes of the polar pack-ice are enormous: great frosty blue islands whose forms melt into the fog; vague, misshapen outlines, with a threat underlying their peaceful appearance; camouflaged fortresses, crystal battering rams, made of eternal ice which loses only a few small ridges in the summer. This, I know, is the ultimate confrontation, the last page of the chapter. Once again, my body stiffens, my whole being is concentrated on a single goal—the goal of winning through.

I have shortened sail and started the engine. My faithful *Williwaw* is already thrusting, dodging, insinuating her way through the gaps in the pack, seeking for the dawn of a most uncertain future. There is no aggression in my heart, and I do not feel threatened by aggression. The battle is an inward one, with elements of a game of skill, a trial of ability, and a test of endurance. The pack is merely the place where the game is played—the obstacle course—and I feel no hostility towards it. Like a climber struggling up a mountain with sweat, toil and suffering, I do not deny the beauty of the landscape.

The hours go by. Rebuffed and dominated by the ice, we have had to move in towards the coast to seek shallower water and fewer obstructions. Mentally, the tension is enormous; physically, I reach the stage of clear and resigned knowledge that I am at the end of my tether. I must stop and recuperate. I have no choice, I'm all in.

24

The Ice Tightens its Grip;
I Almost Lose Mine

The wind has strengthened again this afternoon, but is unfortunately blowing from the north-east, which is not good. It drives the pack towards the coast, and compels me to move into shallow water to shelter from the swell.

As evening comes on I exhaustedly anchor in the lee of a stranded floe. I am happy to think that I shall soon be asleep. Giving up the idea of a complicated meal, I decide to make myself a bowl of hot soup. Having put the water on to boil, I make use of a spare moment to go on deck and look around. I am horrified to see that the floe behind which I am sheltering is not stranded after all, and is coming dangerously close. If it drifts a few metres more, it will press up against the anchor-chain, and I shall not be able to manoeuvre to a position directly over the anchor, which I shall then certainly lose. Immediate action is required; but I have to use all my will power to summon up the necessary energy. We must get away towards the open sea at once, and look for a place sufficiently free from ice to enable me to stop and get a few hours sleep.

An interior dialogue follows, which is conducted with great gentleness. The self which gives the orders shows great understanding for the distress of the self which carries them out. No-one can deny that the latter has done more than his duty and that his defeat is an honourable one. It is not the will that is lacking, but the strength. Total exhaustion has set in. Darkness is gathering fast, and there is not a moment to lose. The pattern formed by the floes has shifted as they run aground; and we must make our way through the barrier that they form before the darkness makes all further manoeuvre impossible.

'Come on, old fellow! Get the anchor up. We never thought it was going to be easy. Come on—breathe slowly and deeply, and measure your movements. Do everything slowly, but resolutely, so that there's no hesitation. Start the engine first of all, and then the winch. Come on, I'll help you.'

The anchor comes up. With eyes stretched wide open to search for a gap between the floes, I slowly make my way out to sea. Then the night comes down, and I heave-to, under mizzen, so as to reduce the risk of the boat getting under way because of the defect in the hydraulic steering-gear. With such help as the radar can provide in a high sea, I have picked out a space among the ice which is sufficiently clear to allow me to drift for a while and get a little sleep. The alarm will wake me up every hour. I note the readings of the echo-sounder, check the depth, and finish making my bowl of soup. After confirming yet again that everything possible has been done for our safety, I flake out.

I must have slept deeply, for I suddenly wake up, worried that I have not heard the alarm. When I check the time, I realise that I have only been in bed for a quarter of an hour. Damn it! I was sleeping so well!

The boat is listing slightly. Tilted against the edge of the bunk, I am deeply aware of every movement caused by the swell. I try to go back to sleep, but my brain is still working and it is a slow business.

'Come on. Up you get. Take a look outside!'

'I can't! I'm too tired; I must sleep . . .'

'Remember the *Karluk*! She was caught in the ice right here.'

'We shan't get caught—the pack isn't dense enough for that. The swell proves it. Let's not look for difficulties. I must sleep, I'm all in.'

(End of discussion.)

The alarm abruptly wakes me up.

'You've got to get up!'

'Yes . . . Just a second . . . I'm coming. Where are my boots . . . and my oilskins?'

'Fasten your collar tightly! Don't put on the light, or you won't see anything outside! Switch on the radar. While it's warming up, check the water-depth and the wind-direction.'

'The wind? Is that really necessary? It's not easy, with the compass as it is.'

'Yes, you'd better check the wind. You need to know which way it's driving us. You can check the direction by the moon.'

'Look . . . I'm tired. I can't see the figures in the tables any more.'

'Put on your glasses; take your time. Come on! where is the almanac? There . . . Right! look at the time . . . 2240 . . . and in

12. The Tasmania Islands anchorage, where we saw the caribou.

13. "We'll never get through, Willy! It's all white ahead!" A difficult moment in the approaches to James Ross Strait.

14. *Williwaw* forced upwards by the formidable pressure of the ice.

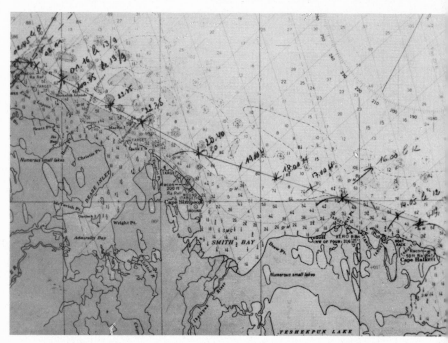

15. My careful plot of the route from Cape Halkett to Point Barrow – a hazardous stretch navigated at the limits of my endurance. (In 1871 the entire American whaling fleet was lost here, and *Karluk* foundered here in 1913.)

GMT? . . . 0840 . . . Right—now look up the hour angle for September 11 . . . Careful, now! Not that column, the other one; not the sun, the MOON . . . That's it, now add the longitude . . . Take your time . . . Now enter it in the Tamaya . . . Declination? . . . Estimated latitude? . . . Well then? What is the azimuth? . . . 152° . . . Excellent—and now for the wind . . . What is its direction relative to the bearing of the moon? . . . Minus 108° . . . 152 minus 108? . . . What does that come to? . . . How much is it? . . . Well? . . . Have you forgotten how to subtract? . . .'

A cold sweat breaks out on my brow. I can see the two numbers clearly enough, but they remain apart from each other. My mind cannot establish a relationship between them, and I realise with horror that I can no longer perform a simple calculation.

'Steady on, my lad; calm down. It's not all that serious.'

'I know, I'm exhausted; I can't do it.'

I had a similar experience a few years ago, in the neighbourhood of Cape Horn, after several long sleepless nights; the weather had been bad and the passage extremely difficult.

I accordingly realise that inability to perform simple mental arithmetic indicates an advanced stage of brain fatigue. I realise that I must get some rest at once. Above all, I must keep out of trouble, for the slightest mishap would cause a serious crisis while my brain is not working properly. Now that I understand my situation, my best course, obviously, is to do as little brain work as possible and to accept my incapacity as a phenomenon which is caused by fatigue and will vanish with it. I must consider the situation in a lucid manner, and try not to feel it as a serious setback.

I solve my problem with the calculator, and discover that the wind is still blowing from the north-east. So I can go back to bed, which I do at once.

During the night the alarm wakes me at regular intervals. Shortly before dawn I see some lights not far away. Strange to say, here is a ship!

I call her up on the radio, and learn that she is the *G.S.I. Mariner*, which is ending her season in the Arctic and is towing a barge towards the Mackenzie River. We exchange a few remarks, and the officer on watch tells me that the most recent weather bulletin reports a 60-knot north-easterly wind at Point Barrow! He strongly advises me to take the shallow-water route, and to keep inshore of the 5 fathom line. He says there is no hope of getting through if I keep out to sea.

'You will run into heavy ice!' he tells me.

I share his opinion, and was in fact already intending to follow the inner route when I moved in towards the coast yesterday evening. I wait for daylight before moving back towards the shore, through the barrier of stranded floes which marks the beginning of shallow water. *Williwaw*'s present position is 6 miles off Cross Island and 180 miles east of Point Barrow. I make a landfall on Cross Island, as planned, and soon afterwards we are on course for Point Barrow, with a force 7 wind blowing from the north-east. We are moving at a good speed. It is very cold, and navigation is difficult. The wind is extremely strong, and the coast is so low-lying that it can only be seen at the last moment.

Anxious to avoid any further excessive fatigue, I plan to anchor behind Thetis Island. Shortly after midday, I set course for the anchorage, looking forward to taking it easy for a few hours. But the water gets progressively shallower as I go on, and I have to reckon with the risk of running aground.

As I want to avoid any additional mental strain at any price, for the reasons already explained, I decide to give up my proposed anchorage at Thetis Island and tackle the crossing of Harrison Bay, where the water is deeper.

Towards 1800 I finally locate Cape Halkett, at a distance of 13 miles. The wind is still strong. Not having any other choice, I decide to anchor near the cape in the open sea. For greater safety, I pay out all the chain. I must sleep this time—and I must eat too, for apart from that bowl of soup, I have not been able to cook anything either yesterday or today.

Snow has begun to fall, and it is infernally cold in the wind. This is not a comfortable anchorage. There is a heavy swell and the strain on the anchor-chain is tremendous. During the night I get up several times to see if everything is holding well in the bows. But alas! when morning comes I discover that the jib has got caught under the anchor-chain, and is quite badly damaged.

Extract from log-book for September 12:

'I got a little sleep last night. At first light I had to weigh anchor. I am very tired!

'I am afraid of fainting. My legs are trembling under me, and only will-power enables me to set sail and drive the boat on.

'At 0800 Barrow is only 61 miles away. There is no ice for the moment. The wind has veered from north-east to east, and then to south-east. It's more than I hoped!

'Snow alternates with drizzle, but visibility remains good. There again, I'm really in luck!

'Conditions have not been all bad these last few days. Even the bad weather had its virtues—at least it came from the right direction!'

Progress continues to be good—better than my hopes. There is still no ice, and Barrow is now only about 20 miles away. The time is 1500. I am really beginning to believe that we have a chance of rounding Point Barrow today. But I am too exhausted to express my joy. I attend scrupulously to the smallest details of navigation. It would be too stupid to make a mistake now!

Soon after 1700 I sight the low, jutting headland with its small lighthouse. Point Barrow, the most northerly point of the United States! At 1745 on September 12 1977, *Williwaw* rounds the cape and enters the Chuckchi Sea. I go on a little into deeper water, and then alter course for Cape Smyth, in the shelter of which I anchor.

All tension gone, I fall asleep immediately—without even having time to savour my achievement. Admittedly, the North-West Passage cannot logically be regarded as complete until we reach the Pacific Ocean; but there is no doubt, as far as ice is concerned, Point Barrow marks the end of the really difficult stretch. Icy Cape, of course, is still to come. This is a low-lying promontory about 110 miles further to the south-west, which is continued out to sea by an extensive reef; it can cause some problems, but they are generally of a less dangerous kind. But we must remember that several ships have found themselves in real difficulties there. In 1778 the great Captain Cook, with his ship *Endeavour*, tried to find a passage into the Arctic from the west coast of North America; and it was this obstacle which finally halted him the following year. I accordingly do not propose to waste any time. We are so late in the season now that the pack will soon reach the coast, and we must not let it catch us there.

But a few hours are neither here nor there. The wind is still strong, and the best plan is to take advantage of the bad weather to recharge one's batteries. I have at last been able to spend a whole night in my bunk, and I have only just got up . . . For the first time for several months, the urge to get on at all costs has abated a little. I am relaxed enough today to take a fresh pleasure in the warmth of the cabin.

There has been a little snow. The frosty portholes do not let in much light, and I find myself dreaming in these shadowy surroundings. The woodwork is very beautiful; fine-grained mahogany, and yellowish, sappy, strong-veined teak. I love wood. It is a noble, living material, and agreeable to the touch. Its warm tones fill the cabin with an atmosphere of gentle peace. The lively texture of mahogany, to which the transparent varnish gives relief and depth, ensnares one's attention; fascinated, the eye follows the fibres which flow through the grain of the wood like the water in the bed of a stream. Its meanderings cannot be taken in at a single glance; and every time that I look at the cabin bulkhead, my eye is caught by some new detail, and the imaginary journey has to begin again and again . . . 'To begin again and again!' These words have a very special meaning for me today.

My arrival at Point Barrow is virtually the end of something which was far more than a chapter in the story of my life—it was almost a reason for life itself. The struggle to reach this point has lasted for years. Now that the dream has become a reality, I realise that the goal can often be less important than the road which leads to it. Despite the anguish, despite the exhaustion, I regret the fact that tomorrow will bring no problems comparable with those of yesterday. Happiness does not come from the absence of troubles, but from the ability to face them.

O eternal relativity of all things, how can we fail to learn your lesson of humility! I know that my voyage will pass into history, that it will be famous, and that my name will remain attached to it. And yet, at the same time, I have just begun to feel the frustration caused by the disappearance of my goal. The more worthy the goal, the greater the frustration . . . So my joy in achievement will never be wholly complete. (Not, at least, until I have given myself a new objective.)

Thus happiness has become identified with action—and ever

more difficult action at that. I was thinking about this a moment ago, as I followed one of the shorter and simpler lines in the grain of the mahogany.

Loss of concentration can often be fatal, and the most dangerous moment of a risky undertaking is when you realise that you have nearly reached safety. This practical reflection brings me down to earth, and I spend the rest of the day on various small repair jobs, so that the boat will be in good condition to carry on with the Passage, which is not yet complete. The Bering Sea, the Aleutian Islands, and the North Pacific all have bad reputations, especially in the autumn. Though I am practically clear of the hazards due to ice, I am undoubtedly about to rediscover those of navigation in heavy weather.

Coming up on deck towards the end of the afternoon, I am surprised to see a mast on the horizon, to the west. Intrigued, I watch it for some time. Before long there can be no doubt about it: a boat is coming towards Point Barrow. What can her destination be? There is no harbour here, and there is no shelter nearer than Herschel Island to the east. Where can she be intending to go now —at the end of the season? I am still more intrigued when I finally realise that the boat is a ketch of fifteen metres or thereabouts. She slowly approaches, comes in behind *Williwaw*, and anchors next to us.

What can this mean? A dinghy is lowered at once, and two men row towards us. They come alongside, head and tail. One of them, an agreeable looking fellow with a fair amount of Eskimo blood in his veins, introduces himself:

'Bob Mackenzie.'

'Ah! from Herschel Island?'

'Yes.'

'Oh! Welcome!'

'Thanks very much. We were expecting to meet you. They told us at Nome, in Alaska, that you were making to round Point Barrow. Congratulations!'

'And you? Where have you come from?'

'Oh! I'm on my way home. We had a lot of trouble on the way, and we've got here later than we expected. We can't wait any longer; its high time we were home.'

Bob Mackenzie and his companion, a young American from

Seattle, come on board for a little, and I learn that Bob bought the boat this summer, and that the journey from Seattle has taken them over three months. They want to take on fuel here at Point Barrow, and are in a hurry to go ashore; but they will come back during the evening. And in fact, shortly afterwards, they are back again, accompanied by the third member of the crew, who is a pure-blooded Eskimo. I give them a drink, and then another. Tongues are loosened, and the conversation goes well. Bob has already slapped me on the back several times. We are friends.

For several minutes I have been wanting to tell him something which is very much on my mind. In the end I can't help it, and I confess that, thanks to a message from the *Pandora II*, I knew that he was away from home and that his young wife was on her own. Then I laughingly tell him that it was just as well for him that the bad weather prevented me from reaching his house. But to my surprise Bob seems very sorry about this and exclaims:

'Oh! Willy! What a pity! . . . She'd have been so pleased! . . . What rotten luck!'

And he tries to insist on my going back to Herschel Island with him so that the three of us can spend the winter together there! Well, whatever next!

I was to find it very difficult to decline the invitation without upsetting him. When we said goodbye, he was still insisting that I should go with him. The Eskimo mind remained a disconcerting puzzle right up to the end.

At about noon on September 14, I weigh anchor and set *Williwaw* free again. As we sail on, the wind is blowing from the north-west, force 5–6. The sea has not yet got up, and sailing conditions remain very good for a large part of the day.

At midnight, I see my first aurora borealis. Brightly coloured curtains, with a predominant steely blue, hang in a velvet sky. Conditions are ideal, for there is no moon, and the aurora covers the entire vault of heaven. The sight makes me feel ill at ease. It is a strange, imperfectly explained phenomenon; it seems to be near at hand, and that makes it appear threatening. It is generally accompanied by a disturbance of the Hertzian waves, which sometimes makes radio communication completely impossible.

As the hours go by, the wind gets up, which affects our progress.

A strong current, setting to the north, also slows us up. Nearly a third of our distance through the water is lost because of this current.

I have a sleepless night. We are having trouble with the compass again—due either to a recurrence of the heeling error caused by listing or to one of the local magnetic disturbances which are characteristic of the Chuckchi Sea—and we have consequently gone off course. I have to tack several times to find a depth compatible with the route on the chart. Soon after dawn, the wind drops, but the swell remains strong all day and the boat rolls a great deal.

I take to my sextant again, and re-establish my position by astronomical observation. Towards 1530 we are 25 miles from Icy Cape. There is no ice, and it seems unlikely that we shall meet with any more.

During the night a violent squall strikes the boat, with snow, hail, and finally rain. It is very windy. The day proceeds without any noteworthy incidents, and in the evening we round Cape Lisburne.

The barometer falls rapidly before steadying at 997 millibars towards 1100 on September 17. I learn through a radio contact that the *Pandora II*, which left the Arctic shortly before us, has met gale conditions in Bering Strait. At 0930 on September 18, I enter in the log-book:

'For about an hour Siberia has been visible on the radar screen. I am rather closer to Russia than I care for, and I luff to make sure that I do not come within twenty miles of her coast. The frontier between the United States and Russia in Bering Strait lies eighteen miles from the Siberian coast.'

I obviously have no wish to be forced to pay a visit to the Muscovites; and so I respect their territorial waters and, to be on the safe side, I keep slightly over towards the Alaskan side.

Finally, at about 1515 on September 18 1977, *Williwaw* rounds Fairway Rock, which marks the end of Bering Strait. The North-West Passage is completed.

25

Epilogue

According to the ideas of those who follow an 'exploit' from afar, success is just a matter of passing the finishing-post. Generally speaking, only the result counts for the public at large; and, if the result is achieved, they cry 'Bravo!' But the man who has achieved the performance is not satisfied with so simple a judgment. For him, the result retains its significance, but the way in which it was achieved is much more important.

The wonderful thing about my great adventure (for the North-West Passage was a great adventure to me), is that my very real satisfaction is in no way disturbed by a retrospective review. I sincerely believe that I have not done badly, for various reasons, some of which I shall mention.

First of all, the Passage was made without harming anything or anybody. No animal has paid for my voyage with its life; I have not destroyed a single flower, nor a plant of any kind. I am proud of this, for it is not always the case—which is a pity. When Amundsen set out for the South Pole, he reckoned that his chance of being the first man to plant the flag of his country there would be greatly increased if he ate his dogs. His calculation was right, and he did reach the Pole. My personal opinion, however, is that no success, however glorious, can justify such a course of action. I am particularly happy to have been able to prove that the mass slaughter practised by certain of my predecessors in the far north was not necessary, and that it is possible to cross the Arctic and other inhospitable regions while maintaining a scrupulous regard for Nature and animal life.

Also, my success has a clear message for the young. The highly organised societies of today, despite all the constraints they impose, are not yet prisons; opportunities for personal adventure still exist for those who really want to take them. (I have received many letters which prove that the spirit of enterprise is still very much alive.) But it is necessary to want such an adventure, perhaps to the exclusion of all else. The man who wants the best car, the largest house, and the most 'in' yacht is unlikely to achieve his goal.

I am also glad to have had an opportunity to show that serious preparation is essential, and that intelligence is our best weapon.

One of my reasons for undertaking this difficult voyage was a long discussion which I once had with a friend of a less rigorous, more happy-go-lucky disposition than myself. I wanted to prove to him that my prudence was well founded. But alas! the sea has swallowed him up, and he is not there to continue our conversation. God knows how much I wish I could have persuaded him! It is my dearest wish that Patrick's fate may help others to become aware of the potential dangers of the sea. This prompts me to emphasise how distressed I am to see so many boats in service which are not capable of standing up to bad weather, so that they really owe it simply to luck that they are still afloat.

The apparent success of a new design of boat means nothing until it has been tested by time.

It has rightly been written that the size of a boat is not necessarily a measure of her sea-going qualities; but it must nevertheless be said—especially for boats of under 15 metres—that, other things being equal, size plays an important role, for it determines the vessel's reserve of buoyancy.

The smaller a boat is, the less water it can take in with impunity. This makes watertightness a most essential safety factor. But unfortunately a small boat requires particularly good ventilation, because of its small interior volume, whereas watertightness requires that openings should be kept down to a minimum. Obviously, this dilemma can only be resolved by a compromise, which itself represents a sacrifice of the safety factor.

Also, while the lines of a boat are important, the strength of its construction is equally so. A leaky drop-keel housing, or a loose chain-plate—the least mishap, in fact—quickly takes on catastrophic proportions in a small boat; for since very little water can be shipped with impunity, there is very little time available for repairs or for life-saving. I have said nothing about the space required for adequate modern equipment. There is no point in lengthening the list! Those of my readers who are capable of understanding will have done so; the others will continue to put their money on their lucky star.

From the point of view of the technique of navigation in high latitudes, *Williwaw*'s voyage is not without interest. Much of what is known about managing small vessels in the ice comes to us from the experience of the late Captain Henry Larsen of the famous Royal Canadian Mounted Police schooner *St. Roch*, who sailed the northern seas for many years. I must of course pay my homage to the very considerable contribution made by the *St. Roch*, and I have already expressed my respect for the men who invariably brought her back to her base in Vancouver in one piece, throughout her twenty-six years of service. But it has to be admitted that the equipment of the *St. Roch* necessarily belonged to an earlier period, and that from this point of view *Williwaw*'s voyage had the benefit of up-dated techniques, involving the use of modern instruments, such as radar and the echo-sounder.

It is my intention to publish some technical articles on this subject before long. The point that I have tried to emphasise in the present work is that the success of the voyage was above all the result of adequate resources of character—without which, it would have been useless to accumulate the necessary knowledge. If, as may happen, some purist of the art of sailing does not find what he is looking for in this book, the explanation will probably be that he is not looking for what is really essential.

The whole voyage caused me only one disappointment. It is of a personal character, and involves Réal Bouvier, of the *J. E. Bernier II*. I am past the stage of having to worry about the press release which appeared on the day of my arrival at Vancouver. In it, Bouvier made a serious insinuation—though I must say it provoked general hilarity—that without the help of the *Bernier*, *Williwaw* would never have completed the Passage. Since then, Jacques Petitgrew, among others, have spontaneously and repeatedly come out with a true account of the matter. In the long run, this fable has harmed no-one but Réal Bouvier himself. I can also disregard the pressure which he tried to exercise, through third parties, on the Canadian authorities to persuade them to hold me up, on the pretext that it would be preferable for a Canadian vessel to arrive first.

What I dislike most about all this is being put in a position where, if I am to set the record straight at all, I must refute certain false claims, which I should have preferred to ignore, because of my friendly feelings towards the other members of the *Bernier*'s crew.

The first point is that (contrary to Bouvier's claims, which have been repeated by the Canadian press) the *Bernier* has not (not at least as I write these words) completed the North-West Passage at all. At the end of her second season in northern waters, the *Bernier* reached Tuktoyaktuk, to the east of the Mackenzie Delta, where she was beached and temporarily abandoned by her crew, who have gone back to Montreal. How can it honestly be claimed that the North-West Passage is completed when a vessel reaches Tuk-toyaktuk, seeing that there are still a thousand miles to cover before arriving at Bering Strait? A very large number of ships have been lost in this part of the Passage.

Strictly speaking, no-one should claim that he has completed the North-West Passage before he reaches the Pacific Ocean. You can, at a pinch, regard the Passage as virtually completed as soon as you are through Bering Strait, since pack-ice, which constitutes the main difficulty of the Passage, is generally absent to the south of the strait. But not before. Dodging Demarcation Bay and Point Barrow is dodging a bit too much!

I imagine that Réal Bouvier must occasionally glance at the Canadian *Pilot Book*. In this case he should know that:

'The North-West Passage spans the North American Arctic from Davis Strait and Baffin Bay in the East to Bering Strait in the West.' (*Pilot of Arctic Canada, vol. I, page 131*). Nothing could be clearer than that. As this definition confirms the one which emerges from the general published literature on the subject, I do not think it is necessary to say any more.

The *Bernier* is therefore (as I write) still 1000 miles from her goal.

In view of that fact, it is of little importance that when Réal complacently records that he was only four days behind me at Tuk he forgets to mention that he started a whole year before me! From a historical point of view, the things that matter are not these wretched quibbles, but the facts; and the facts are that, at the end of her second year in the Arctic, the *Bernier* was still 1000 miles short of Bering Strait. This observation is not without interest, for it puts the difficulty of the Passage back in exact perspective.

The view has already been expressed in various quarters that the speed of my voyage is a proof that it was easy. Nothing could be further from the truth, and I should be sorry to say anything that might support this view. At the risk of being regarded as less than modest, I consider it my duty to emphasise the dangerous, treacherous and highly changeable nature of the ice movements, the enormous force which the pack-ice can exert, the narrowness of the permissible margin of error and the many hidden dangers of arctic navigation.

There are of course other men alive who could achieve the Passage. But that does not mean that anyone could do it. Before I started, I had had more than 50,000 miles' experience with the same boat, and I needed it. I give a realistic picture of the difficulties, not to dissuade any one who possesses the necessary qualities, but to make the others think twice about it. I should be very sorry if the example of my success led to disaster for someone else.

This prompts me to say a few words about the last stage of the voyage. The crossing of the Bering Sea was difficult. The low-pressure area centred on the Aleutian Islands and the Gulf of Alaska was abominably active, producing a close succession of depressions. As the Bering Sea is shallow, the short, choppy waves reminded me of those of the English Channel. There were also low clouds like those celebrated by Jacques Brel.

My kidney stone started to move soon after we were through Bering Strait, and I was hindered at the beginning of the crossing of the Bering Sea by a violent and painful attack.

Finally, on September 25, I reached Dutch Harbour in the Aleutians. The *Pandora II* had left some charts there for me, to enable me to continue my journey.

I received a very warm welcome here, and I was most happy to stay a few days longer than I had intended. On the morning of October 3, laden with numerous useful presents from the American colony, I set sail for Vancouver. My decision to put in there was a natural one, prompted first of all by my regular radio contact with Harry (VE7ZQ). Another factor was my special regard for the epic achievements of the *St. Roch*, so closely linked to the history of this British Columbian port.

Nor could I forget that I had been in contact with Canadians during the greater part of my voyage, and I had come to consider a call at a Canadian port as a natural part of the venture. In view of this, the choice of Vancouver followed automatically. Tempting though it was to abandon the rigours of the North Pacific in autumn for the attractions of southern waters, I set off on an easterly course, battering my way through the rough conditions prevailing at that time of year.

Early on the morning of October 16, I arrived off Tofino, on Vancouver Island. The Canadian Coastguard had offered to meet me with their patrol boat *Racer*; and as I did not have the charts I needed to find my way into port, I accepted. On board the *Racer* were representatives of radio, television and press, together with two distinguished yachtsmen, Ches Richard and Lol Killam, who had been sent by the Royal Vancouver Yacht Club. Their instructions were to ensure that *Williwaw* reached Vancouver in time for the reception which had been organised by the civic and port authorities in conjunction with the Naval Museum (the present home of the *St. Roch*), the Dutch community and the many local yacht clubs.

It was a splendid, unforgettable welcome. The Canadians had been kept informed about my expedition for some weeks past by the media; the whole country, and particularly the city of Vancouver, was passionately interested in my voyage, and dozens of boats and thousands of people were waiting for *Williwaw* with friendly enthusiasm. Among them were the crew of the *Pandora II* and my good friend Harry Beardsell.

There was a reception at the Naval Museum, in the shadow of the *St. Roch*; and later I was received, with Harry, at the City Hall.

The following morning I had breakfast in bed at the Bayshore Inn.

The Arctic suddenly seemed very far away.

Acknowledgments

Wishing to be self-sufficient, I have always avoided asking for help. Certain firms have however chosen to associate themselves with my voyage, whether because they wanted to see their material tried out in exacting conditions, or out of pure interest in exploration or in sporting achievement. In either case, they took the risk of losing their material for nothing, if my venture had been a failure. By trusting me with the equipment in these difficult circumstances, they showed a healthy spirit of optimism and a good deal of faith in myself. For this I thank them most sincerely.

I also thank my friends in various parts of the world who have encouraged me by their sympathy, their generosity, and their help. I cannot mention them all, and if anyone seems to have been forgotten, I hope he will forgive me. It shows that I have found room for him in my heart rather than in my memory.

Before leaving Belgium (in chronological order)
American Garage: installation of diesel engines.
S. A. Tudor: batteries specially adapted to resist extreme cold.
Asahi Pentax Europe: cameras and accessories.
Ets. Krautli S.A.: life-boat, chronometer and anemometer.
Kodak Belgium: photographic film and services.
Lister Belgium: electric generators and accessories.
G.B. Inno B.M.: provisions.
Optique F. Heitz: special sun-glasses.
A. de Koninck: sewing machines.
And my faithful friends Guy Cappeliez, Paul Cordonnier, Alphonse Van Brande, Michel Geerts, Claude and Serge Boucher, and Xavier Hebbelynck.
The Brussels Royal Yacht-Club, and the Lions Club at Wetteren.

During the voyage
The Canadian Coastguard.
The Second Officer of the *John A. MacDonald*, and Katie and Maurice Cloughley. The crews of the *Pandora* and the *Nahidik*, and Bob Mackenzie.

ACKNOWLEDGMENTS

All those who welcomed me at Dutch Harbour. Radio hams in general, and in particular: VE2DDR, ON6FN, ON5YA, ON6GC, VE7ZQ, OX3GW, F6EDF and F6CIU.

At Vancouver
Jack Volrich, the mayor of Vancouver.
The staff of the Naval Museum.
Fred Spoke, the Harbour-Master.
Christian Turkow and Gerard Chabot, the Dutch Consul-General and Consul.
The members of the Royal Vancouver Yacht Club.
The members of the Burrard Yacht Club.
Bayshore Inn Hotel and Marina.
And the following friends: Joy Metcalfe, Liv Kennedy, Harry Beardsell, Lol Killam, Ches Richard, Pat Leslie, Sven Johansson, Pieter Veuger, Ybo Lalau, Stephane Chripounoff.

Those who helped me with the typing of the manuscript:
Madame Lise Brown
Mademoiselle Joëlle Czarniak

Once again, my sincerest thanks to everybody.

Bibliography

American Practical Navigator, N. Bowditch (Washington)
Pilot Book of Arctic Canada, Canadian Hydrographic Service (Toronto).
Arctic Pilot, Hydrographic Dept., Ministry of Defence (London).
Bering Sea and Strait Pilot, Hydrographic Dept., Ministry of Defence (London).
The Friendly Arctic, V. Stefansson (London).
Arctique, enfer de glace, Jeannette Mirsky (Paris).
European Discovery of America, Samuel Eliot Morison (New York).